Viral Marketi[n]

3 Manuscripts in 1 Book, Including: Digital Marketing,
Social Media Marketing and Business Development

Santino Spencer

More by Santino Spencer

Discover all books from the Marketing Management Series by Santino Spencer at:

bit.ly/santino-spencer

Book 1: Marketing Strategy

Book 2: Business Branding

Book 3: Digital Marketing

Book 4: Social Media Marketing

Book 5: Marketing Analytics

Book 6: Content Marketing

Book 7: Business Development

Book 8: Mobile Marketing

Themed book bundles available at discounted prices:

bit.ly/santino-spencer

Copyright

Table of Contents

Book 1: Digital Marketing

7 Easy Steps to Master PPC Advertising, Affiliate Marketing, Email Marketing & Online Retargeting

Santino Spencer

Introduction

Welcome to *Digital Marketing;* whether you are trying to run a business or just up your digital marketing game, you have made a great choice. The seven steps shared within *Digital Marketing* will provide great value to enhance your success. Every business, regardless of size, has to have some type of strategy for digital marketing. Simply going about digital marking without a plan can be very costly and honestly might even hurt your brand.

A business needs to make several key decisions. One of those decisions is about the best way to market their business to keep up with today's technological demands. It is true that businesses have been using technology for several decades now. But if you are running a business, how effectively have you been using that technology to your advantage?

That is where digital strategy comes in. A lot of things have changed since the old ways of marketing businesses through traditional mediums like newspapers, television, radios and magazines. For one thing, customer expectations have changed. It is safe to say that 80% of customers would research a product online before they decide to make a purchase. In fact, customers today prefer to complete the entire purchasing process online. All you have to do is look at Amazon as living proof of that. If you're not out there with a digital strategy that is competitive enough to put you ahead of your competition, you are at risk of losing customers.

People are more mobile today than they have ever been in our history, and every business needs to get on board with an effective, sustainable, results-generating digital strategy. *Digital Marketing* is your introduction into digital transformation for your business. It doesn't matter how big or small your business is, when you have the right strategy, your business can move mountains and leave a profound impact on the world. Let's get started.

Chapter 1: Step 1 - Understanding Why Digital Marketing Is the Future of Your Business

We live in an era of digital innovation and global connectivity, and what a wonderful world it is. We are given more opportunities today than we have ever had, especially from a business standpoint. Who would have thought that several decades ago, online shopping would be the dominant and preferred choice of today's consumers? Who could have predicted that social media platforms would turn out to be one of the best marketing tools out there? The world is changing so dramatically and dynamically all the time that a business needs to adapt to stay on top of its game.

Digital technology holds huge potential for a business. In the last decade alone, **four out of ten jobs** were created in highly digital intensive sectors. Data has become a critical resource with unprecedented velocity and volume. Data also happens to be responsible for powering new strategies, like digital marketing strategies that have made many businesses like Amazon and Apple the number one in their field.

The World Is Changing

For many decades, businesses were founded and they were able to thrive. This was because the landscape on which they founded their business was relatively stable. Brick and mortar businesses were founded, print ads were put out every now and then, and you would hear some businesses being advertised on the radio or television if they had the budget for it. Things started changing in the 90s, and from the 56k modem to broadband, changes began rapidly rolling out from that point on. Before we knew it, the internet was everywhere.

It was connecting people and businesses around the world. Morning, noon, day, or night, people could connect to each other in a matter of seconds. The internet was quickly dissolving borders, and the digital world meant that consumers were quickly gaining power too. The Internet has taken over the world, and every good business out there knows that the digital era is not going anywhere. It is here to stay, and the only option for businesses is to adapt to the demands or risk being out of businesses faster than they can blink. Yes, change happens that rapidly these days.

Without a strategy, your marketing campaigns are going to seem all over the place, like you're trying to do too many things at once. Before you put any kind of content out there, always ask yourself how you can provide as much value that is on-brand with the consumers who are going to buy your product. Unfortunately, many companies still don't fully comprehend the consequences of not having the right digital strategy, and this means they are not making full use of what they have at their disposal. It is a huge missed opportunity, and it is time you started identifying what the right digital initiatives are for your company.

What Is Digital Strategy?

The direction your company takes will determine how successful it is going to be. One wrong turn is all it takes to bring a business tumbling quickly, especially in today's digital landscape where news spreads in a matter of seconds. Before you have time to digest what's happening, news about your business could have reached people halfway across the world already. Both impressive, and alarming at the same time. This only highlights the need for the right strategy, but first, you need to understand *what* digital strategy is.

Building the most impressive website or mobile app is going to be futile if you don't know what you're doing. Before you even begin thinking about ways to make the best website or app out there, you need to think about what your digital strategy is going to be. A digital strategy is a roadmap. A map that will point your company in the direction it needs to take to see results. When applied in the right way, it is going to be the tool that lights up the path you need to take to become part of the digital age. A digital strategy is essentially your *vision* for the company. When you start your business, you need to have some idea of where you would like your company to be. Digital marketing strategies are an inseparable part of your company's core fundamentals. Not only is the right digital strategy going to move your company forward, but it is also going to give your company the steps that it needs to survive in this dynamic and fast-paced tech environment.

Your digital strategy is going to lay out everything that your business would like to accomplish within a certain timeframe. It will streamline your costs and increase your revenue. Since it is your map, it should tell you how to get from Point A to Point B, thus ensuring that your business is never lost along the way. What every company needs is a blueprint for digital transformation. A business, for example, has many internal elements, which include people, applications, data, processes, organization, and culture. They also have external elements like suppliers and vendors that interact with each other to provide value to the customers. Before digital transformation came along, the pace of change has been slow, and this meant that the elements that make up the company did not have to change that fast. These days, everything is so different. The only way for a business to survive is to have that digital strategy map as a guide about the steps and action plans that must be taken next. If you don't know where you are going, then it is only a matter of time before you find yourself at a loss.

One of the most important reasons that make a digital strategy essential to the survival of your business is that it forces you to think about what the needs and expectations of your customers are. When you create a product or service, are you thinking about *them* instead of yourself? It makes you think about the current trends, and this is something a lot of businesses forget to pay attention to when they are more concerned about generating as much profit as possible. You are on a mission to win over your audience. To grab their attention and hold onto it. More importantly, you're on a mission to keep them coming back to your brand for more. A digital strategy is a plan that outlines your market and analyzes your goals to identify which technologies will prove to be the most effective at reaching those goals. Crafting the perfect digital strategy is not rocket science. The elements of your strategy are going to be the hook, line, and sinker that reels in your audience.

A digital strategy is an opportunity for true business development. It is the marketing approach of the future. It encourages businesses to only apply initiatives that stand a chance of making an impact, rather than churn out content for the sake of having something to post on social media. It is important for businesses to think holistically, and that is what a digital strategy can do for you. The right strategy can help to narrow the gap between your company and its digital vision. It is not merely about investing money in the company's online media budget. A digital strategy is an inseparable part of the company's core fundamentals. Marketing without a strategy is like gambling. It might work once in a while and you could get a lucky break, but the odds will never consistently be in your favor if you choose to take a gamble with this approach. There is a better way of getting things done, and this is why you're following this guide. It is time to think of the digital approach.

The Apple Case Study

In 1997, Apple was able to transform its fortune and transform the business, all by having the right strategy. Steve Jobs took all the right steps that made the businesses fit for the future, and it is a perfect example of why digital strategy matters for every business. Jobs and his team saved the businesses from becoming extinct, and his approach to digital strategy is something a lot of businesses can learn from. Jobs made it a point to know the business, know the customers, understand the marketplace and resources, understand where the business stood right now and where it needed to go, and he implemented the right steps and strategies that made Apple what it was today. Jobs was living proof that with the right marketing strategy at the helm of your business, any company can leave behind a legacy.

Apple relied on digital strategy to override their challenges to become the authority in desktop home computers back then. The secret to its continued success was how the business kept innovating to keep up with the emerging trends and what the customers wanted to see. Any Apple user will tell you that the beauty of the products lies in its simplicity and ease of use, and this is why it keeps coming back from more. No matter what the competitors come out with, somehow Apple manages to stay on top, and that is what every business today should strive to do. Be confident and comfortable in your position that you are not threatened by competitors who try to keep up with you. The right digital strategy, as Apple proves, can do that for you.

Chapter 2: Step 2 - How to Create the Right Kind of Content

When you're creating a digital content marketing plan, you want to focus on plans that will help you reach the goals you have for your individual business. The keyword here is *your* goals for *your* business, not someone else's. Avoid trying to copy the digital strategy of another business, because their goals will not be the same as yours. They have their own plans and their own vision for the business, and it is important that you find your own. Your content creation plan should be customized specifically and tailor-made for your individual business needs.

Quality Content Is King

Before you carry out any other part of the marketing process, the first step is to focus on creating the right content based on where your customers are online. The difference between traditional marketing and digital marketing. Traditional marketing relies on tools like radio, television, newspapers, magazines, billboards, direct mail, or any other form of print media to get the message to the consumer. Digital media, on the other hand, consists of tools like social media. Social media has become the number one approach used online these days. Content marketing also includes video creation, articles, blogging), search engine marketing, pay-per-click advertising, mobile marketing, app marketing, and email marketing where ads get sent directly to your customer's inbox. An educated consumer is one that will keep coming back to your business, and the only way to create these educated consumers is to provide them with *quality content.* Quality will always win out at the end of the day over quantity. It doesn't matter how much content you churn out if that content does not add value to the customer.

In the past, a common mistake a lot of marketers and businesses would have made is believing that all they had to do was to get ranked number one on search engines and that was it. Another mistake was believing that getting at list five keywords in their content would be enough to be picked up by Google and the rest would sort itself out. In some cases, that is still true online. But since both the digital marketing landscape and the consumer are now evolving, that is not enough to get the job done anymore. Consumer media consumption trends are continuing to shift dramatically towards more digital content. There will be a time in the future when this form of marketing will no longer be referred to as "digital marketing" because it will be the only form of marketing that exists. Sometime in the future, we'll all simply refer to this as marketing. This is why quality content is going to be the secret weapon that will drive the success of your business online.

Soon, it will not be as simple as a search, click, and buy anymore. Consumers are going to want a lot more from a business before they make a decision. In fact, they are already starting to demand more. The consumers themselves do a lot more research these days before they commit to making a purchase. They will look at reviews and browse social media profiles to gauge other people's comments. They will search for negative reviews and bad comments, check out your competitors and search whether your business has information online that is specific to their needs.

What Type of Content Qualifies As "Great" Content?

Great content is the kind of content that specifically targets a niche group of audiences rather than address a broad, general consumer base. Wait, hang on, doesn't addressing a niche narrow my options? Shouldn't my business be targeting as many people as possible? Yes, but speaking in general terms does not educate the consumer enough. When you're not addressing a specific group of targeted people, you run the risk of creating content for the sake of creating it. It is critical to know *who you are writing for* and *what they are looking for* from your business. Every good writer or creator knows their audience, and this is the reason they are able to generate the kind of content that hits home and generates results.

Great content is the type of content that shares your expertise with your consumers. Your customers want content that is going to make their lives easier, help them make or save money, and content that will tell them how to make their lives easier. Your customers are looking to you to educate, entertain, and provide value through your digital content. If they can't get this from you, they'll go to your competitors for the answers they seek. The whole point of creating content to fill up the online space with your presence is because you need to convince your customers why they should pick you and not your competitor. You're not the only business out there doing what you do. Staying relevant and keeping your customers loyal is about being able to meet and fulfill the needs that they have. If they don't get it from your business, they will get it from your competitors, and there is no amount of marketing you can do that will keep your customers with you if you are not meeting their needs. This is where content comes in. Great content helps you get more leads, make consistent sales, build your reputation, and put your business on the map the way Apple did.

Quality content is the kind of content that will help you build a name for yourself while making money online. It is the best way to attract people to your business online, build a relationship with them, and add value that keeps them loyal to your business. The Internet world is all about content, and the kind of content you provide will be the defining difference between you and your competitors.

The Type of Content You Should Be Generating

One of the most popular types of content is video. Video marketing experts will tell you that everyone should be creating more videos. Videos are popular among consumers because they have a much higher entertainment value and they are a lot more enjoyable to watch. A well thought out video can do more wonders for your business marketing plan than any conventional marketing tool ever could.

Other types of content you should be creating for your business include any of the following:

- Written content (Tweets, Instagram and Facebook posts, articles, and more)
- Short blogs and long blogs
- Podcasts
- Social media
- Infographics
- Newsletters and copywriting
- Live Streams
- Interviews
- Ebooks

Basically, you want to produce the kind of content that is engaging, interesting, attractive, informative, and fun. The type of content you choose would depend on what your niche audience prefers. Some audiences might prefer to watch content because they happen to be more visual, while others might prefer to listen to a podcast. Ultimately, your content needs to tell a story, a story that is good enough to win the hearts and minds of your audience. Is creating the kind of content your audience demands time-consuming and a lot of hard work? Yes, it can be. Is it going to be worth it? Yes, it absolutely will be worth all the hours you put in once you start seeing results.

Who Churns Out the Content?

That would be a Content Marketing Specialist, a role that was created specifically for this digital era. This person would be in charge of social media channels and monitoring overall online traffic. They would work closely with the Digital Marketing Manager, or sometimes take on both roles, and be responsible for marketing a business's products or services using digital channels to meet consumers. The key objective is to promote the brand as effectively as possible through various forms of digital media with the help of digital technology. As a content creator, it is their job to keep track of the content that goes online and how frequently it gets posted online.

Do you need to hire a specific person to fill the role? Yes, you do because creating quality content requires time and the willingness to invest in this special skill set. Posting quality content that drives sales is *very different* from uploading content the way you normally would on social media. Uploading a picture of your latest product or service because it's "cute" or "looks good" is not going to get you very far with your customers. They might be entertained, but they will easily forget about your content five seconds later, that is how quickly things can change online. That is why this role was created specifically, once businesses began to realize how valuable creating quality content online is and what a difference it makes to the business. These specialists frequently work with various departments within a company to ensure campaigns are launched on the right foot and on track with the business goals. The Content Marketing Specialist has to be in touch with all the different points and understand what kind of content needs to be in place to create a conversion. The specialist and the Digital Marketing Manager will be at the forefront of various digital projects that are carried out for the business.

Chapter 3: Step 3 - Preparing Your Digital Strategy

Whether you're just getting started, or you're already established business, everyone can benefit from having the right digital strategy on their side. If you are going to be competitive in today's business landscape, a clear digital marketing strategy is a must. This goes without saying. After all, no one ever goes into battle without equipping themselves with the best armor they can get. The best part about digital strategies is how they can be applied to *any* sort of business. It doesn't matter if you're selling coffee, shoes, tennis rackets, baseball bats, hats, food, drink, and more, every business can soar to the next level when they have a proper strategy outlined to get them to where they want to be.

How do you go about building your digital marketing strategy? By implementing the following steps in the right order.

Step 1: Set Clear Objectives

You want to be clear from the start what your objectives are. This is the foundation upon which the rest of your plan is going to be built. If your digital marketing strategy was a house, the objectives would be the foundation that must be laid out first before the rest of the framework can fall into place. Defining goals and objectives early on will go a long way in helping to separate data that will be useful to your business's development from data that isn't relevant. Now, what are some of the objectives you have in mind? Are you trying to:

- Raise more brand awareness?
- Generate leads that turn into concrete sales?
- Drive sales for an eCommerce product you are selling?

No matter what those objectives are, they need to be as definitive as possible. When you're drafting them out, be sure to include as much detail as you can. The more specific your objective, the better. It is important to define what your marketing objectives are from the start as this will help you determine what your campaign should be about. Setting specific marketing objectives keeps you focused on your goals. By centralizing certain measurement metrics, you have the ability to keep better track of your accomplishments and goals. For example, if one of the marketing objectives is to influence and increase sales, then you need a metric that defines what the successful target should be like. Objectives can be categorized by measurability indexes, relevancy, and time. When the objectives are clearly defined, it will help you determine how you are going to measure your success.

Measuring and tracking your success throughout your marketing campaign is an essential part of the process. By tracking your progress at every stage, it will help you see whether you are on the right track to meeting your objectives. With a proper tracking system in place, you get to determine if your campaign needs to be tweaked along the way when it seems to be veering off course.

Step 2: Understand the Audience You Are Trying to Target

The better you understand your audience, the more successful your campaigns will be. Some simple things you can try to outline your audience when you are preparing your digital strategy includes the following:

- Is your target audience male or female?
- What is the specific age group you are targeting?
- Is your niche audience young or old? Are they retired or working?
- What is their geographic location?
- Which states or countries do they live in?
- How much time do they spend online?
- What type of social media platforms are they the most active?
- When do they spend the most time online? Is it in the morning, afternoon, late evening, or nighttime?
- Do they have specific behaviors that are unique to them? For example, some audiences prefer to shop online as their main mode of getting what they want. Other consumers might like to start their searches online, and then go to the physical store to get what they need.

The details matter, especially if you are working on a limited budget. You want to be as conservative as possible with your resources, making sure they are invested in the right kind of audience who will, in return, give you the results that you want. The little details that often get overlooked happen to be the very details that will create the most successful digital marketing campaign you have ever done.

Step 3: Figure Out Your Messaging

This is a very crucial stage of your digital strategy preparation. When your audience is starting to get to know your business, there will be certain things they are evaluating you on. For example, if you were in the market to purchase a house. What would be the criteria you look out for? The price, for one thing. The second would be how central the house is to schools, shops, and other basic amenities you might require. You might also look at the different financing options you have available to you, depending on the company that you choose to seal the deal with. You would also consider the type of home, whether it is going to be a one-bedroom, two-bedroom, or family home if you come with a family. Why is all of this information important? Because it is going to determine how your message comes across.

Different messages are going to resonate very differently, depending on your audience. Therefore, part of your digital marketing strategy should be to test out a few messaging systems to see what works best. Your messages should create a value proposition, and this is where you would hit your consumers with the benefits and why they should choose your business over your competitors. Another approach to messaging would be to go with the social proofing route, where you disperse messages that contain statistics and numbers if this resonates better with your audience. For example, messages that say, *"Thirty percent of people you know have purchased from us,"* or *"Ninety percent of the people who have chosen us have experienced success."* Numbers could add credibility to your brand, and it stands out well when you are trying to market online. Another type of messaging approach to consider would be to use the *FOMO* approach. *FOMO* stands for the *Fear of Missing Out*, and since a lot of people are afraid of missing out, this is definitely something you can utilize to your advantage. It all depends on what your audience responds best to, and the only way to find out for sure is to test it.

Step 4: Determine Your Channels

Once you have figured out your objectives, who your audience is, and the type of messaging approach you're going with, the next step is to think about which channels they spend most of their time on. In the online world, where would you be most likely to find your target audience? Think of this approach as if you were the cool kid who was trying to throw a party. You want everybody to come over and you want them to have a good time. You want them to know that your house is *the place* to be. But since these kids are not at your house yet, you want to go to *where they are* and invite them over. If they're hanging out at the library, the basketball court, or the mall, then you are going to head over to the library, the basketball court, and the mall and tell them why they should be over at your house right now. In this case, your party would be your website.

The channels to consider sourcing for your potential customers include social media, the obvious choice, and there are a lot of social media channels out there where you can start building relationships with your audience and bring them back to your website. Other resources to turn to include search engine marketing and this consists of paid searches and organic searches like SEO on search platforms like Google, Bing, and Yelp. Email and affiliate marketing are also options to consider scouring for potential audiences.

Step 5: Think About Your Content

Following all those previous steps in order will lead you to the final part of your digital marketing strategy preparation. Thinking about the kind of content you want to create. What kind of content does your audience prefer to consume? Do they like videos, or do they prefer photos? Do they like to listen to audio, or would they prefer to read about it in an article or blog post? Do they prefer to interact in forums? Once you understand who your audience is and what the best channels to reach them are, you can understand the context of the type of content they are consuming. This will give you the information you need to build your content around what *they want*. This is how you produce *quality content* that will win them over to your side and keep them loyal to your business because they love the way you seem to be able to connect with them and connect in a way that your competitors haven't been able to do yet.

Chapter 4: Step 4 - A Guide to Budgeting

Every business knows that to get sales, you need to promote your business. The question is, *what should you be spending your money on?* A budget, and the ability to stick to that budget, is what keeps your company afloat. Since funds are limited, you want to be certain that you are spending your money in all the right places. There is nothing worse than blowing through your resources only to realize at the end that it didn't give you the results you wanted. To fix that problem so it never happens to your business again, you need a marketing budget.

What Is a Marketing Budget?

A marketing budget is simple. It is how much money you intend to spend on your advertising material within a specified timeframe. For example, if you had $500 dollars to spend within six months, that is your marketing budget. marketing. With big brands, they have the advantage of bigger name recognition, bigger budgets and of course a team to post across multiple channels, create, and curate beautifully designed posts and generally have more influencers who would want to be connected to the brand. Social media is by far the most popular platform utilized because of how deeply ingrained it is in all our lives. It's almost impossible to find anyone who owns a smartphone these days who does not have at least one social media app installed.

Getting the most bang for your buck is also going to come down to strategy. Digital marketing is broken down into a few categories:

- Branding
- Content marketing
- Email marketing
- Affiliate marketing
- Social media marketing and promotion
- Search Engine Optimization (SEO)

Ideally, you should test out the different channels before you settle on the best one for your business. This rule should apply even if you have a limited budget to work with. Your budget allocation is going to depend on what your primary goal is. If your primary goal is to improve brand awareness, that is where the majority of your budget should be allocated. If your primary focus is customer acquisition, then that will be your primary focus. It is better to find the very best option rather than gamble or guess what is going to work best, only to realize that it didn't.

This is why you need to set your marketing goals before you tackle the budget portion of your strategy. You need to know *where you want to go* before you can decide on the best approach to get there. As with everything else when it comes to your digital strategy, the best goals are the ones that are very specific. An example of a poor goal would be *I want to make my business more popular*. This is an example of a poor goal because it is far too vague, making it impossible to measure your results. An example of a good goal would be *I want to obtain 200 new leads every month.* This is a much better goal to set because of the measurable specifics available. It is measurable with numbers, it is specific, and it is time-bound. A common practice would be to create about two to three marketing goals and spread your budget between them. With a clear objective in mind, you will be able to predict the promotional channels that will work best.

The Benefits of Going Digital

One piece of good news with digital marketing is how much more cost-effective advertising your business, products, and services have become. For one thing, the relatively low cost, especially on social media, means that marketing online is now easily accessible to anyone, even if you have a small budget to work with. This is one of the biggest pros when it comes to digital marketing, especially when you think about how costly traditional marketing methods are. A lot of social media platforms are free or require a very minimal start-up cost. For a new business that is just starting to get off the ground and build a name for itself, this is almost free, with some advanced features that require payment.

Digital marketing is by far one of the most affordable tools that you can tap into to build momentum and a steady customer flow on a budget. The wide audience reach, of course, goes without saying. No other marketing method out there will allow your business to reach millions and billions of customers around the world in a matter of seconds. Before the digital age came about, it was not possible to upload content that is seen almost instantaneously by an eager customer who is waiting on the other side of the globe. What a marvelous opportunity digital marketing has provided us with. It has opened a lot more doors, especially for smaller businesses who might have struggled with advertising before this since they didn't have the kind of spending power bigger powerhouse brands did.

What is even better is that with digital marketing, we now have access to instant results, something that was not possible with traditional advertising before. These built-in analytics tools in social media applications allow companies to easily track their progress on a daily, weekly, and monthly basis, and this is essential in marketing. You must always know how your business is performing. With real-time results, you could make changes almost immediately to your campaigns, ensuring that your precious budget dollars are not going to waste.

Steps to Begin Creating Your Budget

Once you have a clear objective in mind, it is time to get to work creating your marketing budget. Most marketers would recommend that you spend about five percent of your total budget on maintaining your current position, and twelve percent of your total budget on growing your business if this is one of your marketing goals. Extreme cost-cutting and marketing are two things that simply do not go together under any circumstance. While it may be painful for companies to fork out large sums of money, it is important to keep the bigger picture in mind. In marketing, you will get what you pay for and cutting costs without thinking of the long-term benefits is one way that a business will end up with the short end of the stick. It can be tempting to try and save as much money as possible, but it is also important to be realistic. If you want the results, you have to be willing to spend sometimes.

It is natural for businesses to want to maximize profit and gravitate towards what the most budget-friendly deal may be. But in this instance when it comes to building the reputation of a brand, being budget-friendly may not necessarily be the best way to go. Again, you get what you pay for in marketing, the more you invest, the more benefits you stand to reap. In a highly competitive niche, you might have to spend up to twenty percent of your overall budget on your advertising. If this is your very first marketing campaign, a safe approach would be to take $100 dollars to begin testing the different channels as you start to familiarize yourself with how marketing in the digital space works.

Once you've done all, these are the next few steps to take to start creating your marketing budget:

- *Step 1: Choosing Your Channels* - There is no definitive answer about what marketing tools are going to work best for you. It would depend entirely on your preference, business needs, goals, and marketing capabilities. As a beginner, the safest channels to start with would be Instagram, Facebook, and Google Shopping. Your focus niche would play a factor in your channel of choice too. For example, if you were selling enamel pins, the best approach would be to promote those visually. In that case, Facebook, Pinterest, and Instagram would be the best channels to market your products. If you were selling sports or exercise equipment, on the other hand, the promotional channels you would probably aim for you would search engine optimization. Facebook advertising and Google AdWords will help too.

- *Step 2: Divide Your Marketing Budget* - Now that you have your goals, budget, and channels of choice, it is time to divide your marketing budget. How should you share your limited budget between these channels? One way to tackle this would be to set a daily budget for each channel. As a newcomer, opt to start with Instagram Ads and Facebook Ads. Since Facebook and Instagram now belong to the same company, this has the added perk of being able to advertise on both platforms for a better cost-effective solution. For example, if you have $100 in your budget to split between these channels to advertise your enamel pins once again, you can choose to spend $60 dollars on Instagram and $40 on Facebook or vice versa. It would depend on where your target audience is. With that same $100, if you are splitting your budget between Google AdWords and Facebook Advertising to market your sports equipment, you could choose to spend $70 on Google AdWords and $30 on Facebook. These numbers are just a guide because you can choose to split your budget in the best way you see fit. You could even split your budget evenly 50-50 on two different platforms if you wanted. You will have to play around with the figures, in the beginning, to see where you're getting the most results between the two channels. Once you've figured out that perhaps Instagram is more popular than Facebook, for example, you can allocate more funds toward Instagram.

- *Step 3: Testing Your Campaign* - No one can guarantee that their advertising campaign is going to work perfectly right from the start. It is all about testing your options, making tweaks and adjustments along the way as you go. This is why every campaign should be tracked, monitored, and analyzed every step of the way. Reddit is one example of a good source to use for tracking since it shows you what people are talking about and what is the latest topic or subject that is going viral. You might stumble across some pretty good ideas to use in your campaign.

- *Analyze Your Results* - The best way to make the necessary changes would be to analyze your results. Once the campaign is over, it is time to analyze your results to see whether your marketing goals were successfully met. The best way to do this would be to use UTM codes, otherwise known as an *Urchin Traffic Monitor.* The UTC codes can be used to track where the source of your traffic is coming from. Email marketing software, on the other hand, can be used to track and measure your click rate, open rate, number of new subscribers, and unsubscribers. As for social media channels, use the built-in analytics to measure the number of shares, likes, and comments on your content. All these data will reveal whether you have achieved your goal, and if you haven't, you will at least have an idea or what needs to be changed for the next campaign to get better results.

Chapter 5: Step 5 - Why Email Marketing Automation Is a Game Changer

Why does automation work so well for email marketing? Email marketing automation has been the trend for the last few years.

What Is Email Marketing Automation?

Have you ever wanted to learn about the behavior of your customers? Why do they make the purchases that they do? Why do they remain loyal to a brand? When are they most likely to make a purchase? These are all questions that can be answered through email marketing automation. Email marketing automation, in a nutshell, is a solution that allows your business to automate its repetitive tasks. In doing so, you free up more time to focus on the other aspects of running a business. Automation solutions allow you to align your marketing efforts with sales and empower both teams to achieve their targets without wasting time on manual drudgery. A simple way to define this solution would be using software and technology to aid sales and marketing by automating simple tasks so they can be performed more effectively by using multiple channels. Automation gives you all of the tools you need to ensure that your communication with your customers is both relevant and focused.

Automation is a game-changer because it unlocks a very unique opportunity. The opportunity to learn about how your customers are interacting with the content that you send them. You get to quickly deduce what your most popular products and services are, how long it takes them to make a purchase and even the time of day or specific day that they prefer to receive their emails. For example, maybe your target customers prefer to get their emails on a Friday when the weekend approaches and they are in the mood to spend a little.

How Email Marketing Automation Will Benefit You

Among the many reasons why email marketing automation is a game-changer include the following:

- ***You Get to Send Emails as Soon as Someone Joins Your List*** - Presumably, your website would have a signup form that encourages visitors to your website to subscribe to your newsletter or for updates from your business. Automation can be used as a tool to send a chain of emails (not all at once, of course). The benefit of this is that you get to communicate with the recipient when their interest in your services or products is at its peak. Automation tools make it easier for your business to acknowledge and thank your customers promptly without needing to invest additional manpower into that effort.

By automating simple and repetitive messages that you've probably already written, you can explode engagement among prospective customers, existing customers, and when you onboard new customers. It can help your business significantly if you provide your customers with clarity right from the start, especially when it comes to cold leads who might not be familiar with the entire scope of what your products and services can do to better their lives. The gap between when the customer first signs up and when they receive their first email communication from you is the period when they are most likely to lose interest in your services and move on. This is why you need to act quickly if you want to win them over. Since you can't sit behind the computer and monitor your emails 24/7, automation is the best way to go.

- *You Can Send Emails on Significant Dates* - With automation, you get to send emails to your customers on significant dates. For example, when you send them an email with a special discount exclusive just for their birthday. Simple gestures like these can go a long way toward helping your customers feel valued. It will make them more likely to retain their loyalty to your brand. You get to make your job much easier too by sending the same email to multiple people at once automatically. This is a lot more effective than having to contact them one by one. An email list along with a list of existing marketing material gives your business an edge over those who are not using this system because if you play your cards right, you could turn these customers into more than just email readers. You could turn them into paying customers.

- *You Can Send Chain Emails That Are Timed* - Maybe part of your campaign includes an email series, but you know that flooding the inbox of your customers with one email after another will only turn them off. Or worse, they could hit the unsubscribe button because they are annoyed by the flood of emails they are getting from you. Timing is crucial here, and you want to catch your customers at just the right time so they don't find your emails annoying and persistent. You can send your customers a chain of emails, but time them so they are adequately spaced out. This approach is called drip marketing, and it is extremely effective when utilized correctly. The ability to plan ahead will allow for more control over your marketing campaigns.

- *You Can Send Your Customers Decision-Based Emails* - Another fantastic benefit of email marketing automation is that you get to create dynamic campaigns. These campaigns can be used to route your customers down different paths depending on how they interact with your initial email. For example, you can send a customer an email that promotes three different products offered by your business. Each product has a click-through link that directs them to your website. The automation process will send your customer another follow-up email. This email is going to be different, depending on which of the three products your customers end up clicking on. This will help you point your customers in the direction of the exact information they want to see. That's the beauty of automation. It will segment your data for you and generate the best possible results for your business. Without having to do this manually, you're saving *a lot* of time.

- ***Your Email Campaigns Will Be More Consistent*** - This is the highlight of why email marketing automation is a game-changer. With automation, you now get to send email marketing campaigns that are consistent. With the limited time we have for marketing these days, given that there are other aspects of the business that must be looked after too, there is only so much you can do in a day. Automation is here to make your life much easier marketing-wise.

The advances with automation mean you can set up long email chains that can go at timed intervals over several months. This gives you the flexibility to create all of your marketing campaigns when you have the time to do it. This way, even if you are busy, you ensure that you always have something going out to your customers and there is never a lull between your email communication with them. Yes, email marketing automation is indeed a fantastic tool for generating consistent email marketing campaigns. By automating a lot of your workload, it gives you more time to focus on other supporting marketing strategies you could utilize to boost your business even further.

- ***It Dramatically Increases Your Conversion Rates*** - All of the previous points culminate in this benefit, and that is email marketing automation can dramatically increase your conversion rates. You are building loyalty, relationships, and with consistent, well-timed emails, you ensure that you are always on their radar. More importantly, you are sending them emails based on what they *want to see,* not what you think they should see. This will exponentially increase the chances of your customers buying from you when you give them what they already want.

Automation makes your marketing incredibly refined, and this is absolutely a game-changer compared to the marketing methods of old. Moreover, this is going to minimize the number of unsubscribes you get to your emails when you are not spamming your customers with unnecessary content they don't want to see. If your content remains relevant to your customer, the number of people unsubscribing from you is dramatically reduced. Receiving emails that are not relevant to their preferences is one of the biggest reasons why customers end up removing themselves from your email list or marking you as spam content. Neither of which are favorable outcomes.

Through email marketing automation, your customer retention rates are going to go up significantly. By regularly communicating with your target audience, you are building a long-term relationship with them. This means they will continue to purchase from you after that all-important first sale. Retention rates with your long-term customers will outweigh the customers with whom you market to with one-off email blasts.

No doubt about it, email marketing automation is one tool you must have in your digital strategy arsenal. With access to information of this depth and specificity, there is no telling how far you can take your business if you apply the knowledge that you learned correctly. Ultimately, this is going to translate into more sales, and we all love to see the sales rolling in.

Chapter 6: Step 6 - Tell A Digital Story That Sells

What was your favorite story when you were younger? Perhaps it was one of those fairy tale classics or a story that your parents read to you when you were growing up. Stories last through the ages because they evoke emotion. When you think about your childhood stories and hear them again, you feel that same rush of emotions. When you recall a happy memory and the story that went along with it, if you closed your eyes, in your mind you can feel all those same emotions that you felt back then. Almost as if the story was happening all over again. Now, imagine if you could channel the power of a compelling story into your digital marketing campaigns? How powerful would they be?

When taken as a whole, the entire digital storytelling process can appear overwhelming if you haven't done it before. The key is to break the process down step-by-step to make it easier. Once you get the hang of it, digital storytelling isn't that bad. The digital world is here to stay, and digital storytelling is one of the many new marketing concepts that has become popular. It is imperative that businesses keep up with the changes if you don't want to be left behind. Nokia is a very real example of what happens when a business underestimates the impact of the digital era and what refusing to change with the times can do. From being the best-selling brand around to a brand that is now almost obsolete, Nokia's refusal to change ultimately led to its downfall and it was because the management underestimated the importance of the digital era that this costly mistake happened to begin with. Perhaps if they had been willing to adopt these new marketing approaches, like digital storytelling, things might have been different. Competition is fierce, and your organization needs to be ready to react to Plus, the benefits that stand to gain from a digital marketing standpoint will make the time you invest in this process worth it.

What Is Digital Storytelling?

A digital story is typically shown in video format. It combines audio and video clips to tell your brand's story. Digital storytelling means using multimedia tools to bring your company's story to life. The best part about digital stories is how versatile they are. You could tell a story on a wide range of topics, and the possibilities of enthralling your customers are endless. Digital storytelling is by far one of the most engaging ways to connect with your audience. All you need is creativity on your side. Some examples of digital stories you could tell include:

- Explaining a concept.
- Sharing or reflecting on a personal experience that you or your business went through.

- Sharing the story of how your business was born, something the customer is always curious to get to know.
- Recreating a historical moment in your company's history.
- Presenting the benefits of your product in a unique way.
- Announcing the launch of a new product or service.
- Presenting a case or making an argument.

Why Would You Create A Story?

After all, isn't it less work to simply snap pictures or record short videos and post them with an entertaining caption. Yes, but your results are not going to be as impactful. Your social media profile is the face of your business, but that's not the only aspect of your business. Telling your story is how you get your audience to know you, to love you, and to trust you. It is not about constant promotions anymore. Now, you need to connect with your audience on such a deep level that they look forward with excitement to your next big product launch. Presenting information and facts by talking numbers and stats all the time is dry and not as appealing or engaging. If you truly want to capture the hearts and minds of your audience, you need creativity on your side.

What better way to tell your business's story than through one of the most expressive methods out there?

The Process of Creating Your Story

A digital story would usually last about two to three minutes (although it could be longer, depending on the medium you are publishing your story), but despite its short length, there is a lot of work that goes into creating this simple story:

- ***Step 1: The Brainstorm*** - The first part of the process involves brainstorming your story ideas. This is where you might spend quite a bit of time thinking about what you would like to present to your customers. What would make a compelling story about your company? It is safe to say that if you're already thinking about creating a digital story, then you probably have a concept in mind already. All that is left is to fine-tune it. The best kind of story is the ones that have a human-interest element in them.

- ***Step 2: Creating Your Script and Storyboard*** - Once you've thought about the story you would like to share; the next step is to come up with your storyboard and your script. When you're preparing to write your script, you will need to give some careful thought to what you would like your story to accomplish.

   What is the goal you want your audience to walk away with once they have reached the end of your story? What result do you want your story to generate? The script and the storyboard will lay out how the story is going to unfold as the finished product. This is by far the best way to go because writing out your script and story will help you organize your thoughts.

Since the ideal length of a video should be no longer than five minutes, plan your content accordingly. You'll probably go through a few drafts before you finalize the finished script. Keep it simple, though, because you don't want to risk overwhelming your audience with information. About the storyboard, if you're wondering whether this is a step you should bother about, the answer is yes.

Think of your storyboard as a sketch. This sketch is going to be focused on how you want to organize your content and your story. With a storyboard, you have a way to define the parameters of your story based on the time and the resources that you have. It helps to give your script some clarity and a focal point. This way, you can determine if your story is on the right track the way that you envisioned it *before* you start shooting.

When you've got some clarity and a focal point, it gives you a much better idea about what kind of medium you should use for your story. The storyboard part of the process is critical because this is where a lot of your initial concept is going to get worked out. This is where you define the visuals you need to create to effectively convey your story to your audience.

A good movie is never without a storyboard, after all, and you should definitely think of your story as a mini movie. A short, but sweet clip that needs to entertain your audience in under five minutes. If your story isn't compelling or good enough to win them over in under five minutes, you lose out on making a sale. Refine and polish your script as much as possible before you move on to step number three.

Step 3: Creating Your Video - If you thought the brainstorming part was time-consuming, wait until you get to the video creation bit. This is going to be the most demanding step by far. Depending on what your script of storyboard entails, there are several things you might have to do. Recording voice-overs, gathering, and creating images or video clips, and finally, you would choose your music and sound effects.

Once all three steps have been completed, you will put together your finished product and present it for the digital world to enjoy.

Quick Tip About Attention Spans

An online user these days has a very short attention span. Quite literally, the attention span lasts only a few seconds. Many social media and internet users these days, have the attention span of a goldfish. It is going to take something *really* intriguing and compelling to make them pause on your video long enough to watch it all the way through. The internet is a wonderful tool, but it also happens to be a very distracting tool.

While watching a YouTube video, for example, some users might pause the video at different intervals to stop and check their phones if they receive a notification. Sometimes, they might not even need a notification at all, they simply pick up the phone out of habit to scroll through aimlessly for a while.

Since your average audience is probably going to consume several other forms of digital content *while* they are watching your story, it is safe to say that you should absolutely invest the time to make your story as interesting as you possibly can. This is the age of social media where the average attention span of a viewer lasts approximately less than 3-minutes before they lose interest and move on to the "what's next?"

Your audience wants to get to the content they're looking for quickly, and they simply don't have the time or the attention span to be reading through your detailed description or blog post. This only proves a point as to why digital storytelling is your best-selling point.

You only have seconds or minutes to deliver the key message of your marketing campaign, and those minutes need to count. The information should be both entertaining and easy to digest. This means your digital story cannot be anything too complicated. If it is too difficult to understand, the truth is, most of your audience might not even bother. We live in a generation where everyone wants things to be as simple as possible.

Chapter 7: Step 7 - Tracking Your KPI and Metrics

Now that you have the bulk of your strategy complete, there is one final matter that needs looking into. Using numbers to prove that all your hard work and efforts have been paying off. This is where *Key Performance Indicators (KPIs)* come in. Let's jump right into it.

What Are Digital Marketing KPIs?

A KPI is a metric. This metric is used to help you check in on the progress of your projects. This will help you confirm whether all that effort you put in the first six steps of the process is indeed paying off. It will also give you an indication of how to bring in more money to your business. SMART Goals have been around for a long time. The reason they are still relevant today is that they're based upon an effective concept that produces results. SMART Goals are a guide for how you should plan your marketing campaign using those five indicators the letters stand for. The five key indicators you need to help you plan marketing and advertising campaigns that win every time. The best KPIs out there are the ones that follow the SMART Goal framework. This means that the KPIs should be:

- Specific (S)
- Measurable (M)
- Achievable (A)

- Relevant (R)
- Time-Bound (T)

For example, let's say that you set a target for yourself to achieve ten thousand new followers for your Instagram account. If you wanted to convert that to a *SMART KPI,* you would frame the goal like this:

"The aim of my business in the next six months (time-bound) is to influence the sales I make through Instagram (relevant). The goal is to grow the number of followers on the Instagram account from five hundred followers to ten thousand followers (specific and measurable). I aim to do this by partnering with influencers and organizing giveaways (achievable)."

Notice how specifics and details will always play a role in your overall digital strategy. In almost every step of the process, the more details you include, the better it will be.

How Do I Choose the Best KPIs for My Brand?

As a rule of thumb, the best kind of KPIs is the ones that remain the most relevant to your brand, your company, your team, and the current marketing project that you are working on. KPIs are not going to remain the same throughout your entire business lifespan. No business will ever start and stick to the same KPIs and never change them. To figure out what the best KPI for your overall digital strategy is, you need to ask yourself this question: *If you had to focus on just one thing, what would it be?* You could brainstorm a list of ideas you have in mind, and then pick one using that question as a guideline.

The KPIs that you track should only be the ones that you are actively trying to influence. For example, if your KPI was to grow your Instagram following but you're not planning projects to make it happen, then it might not be the best KPI after all. A KPI should always reflect what your current priority is, and this is going to change with each marketing campaign that you run.

How Do I Track My KPIs?

The simplest way to do this would be to set up a spreadsheet in Excel or Google sheets. You would then manually add the numbers at the same time every week. This will give you a week by week comparison for you to gauge if your campaigns are progressing the way that you hoped. The numbers that you need for your spreadsheet can be pulled from sources like Google Analytics, email marketing platforms that you use, or other marketing tools that you are relying on.

It sounds like a time-consuming task, doesn't it? A quick tip to make tracking your KPIs a little easier if you are really pressed for time would be to do it based on the following guidelines:

- Track your KPIs weekly only when it is very important to the business or a significant change needs to be made to your strategy. One example of when you would track your KPIs weekly would be when you are trying to grow your email list.

- Track your KPIs monthly if you want to see an overall snapshot of how much growth percentage you achieve per month. An example of when this method works is when you want to see if your customers are starting to spend more time on your website. This is because variables could skew the numbers if you were to do short-term tracking.

- Track your KPIs quarterly if you have one of those campaigns that require you to wait a while before you start to see any visible results. This approach works best for SEO-based strategies since these strategies often take several months to play out. Therefore, better use of your time would be to track these numbers quarterly instead of weekly.

Your Most Important Metrics

There are going to be a lot of metrics that you can look at when attempting to track the progress of your digital marketing campaigns. The question is, *what* are the most important metrics that you should be paying attention to? For every campaign you run, it is crucial to measure its effectiveness. The goal of a successful marketing campaign is to make it self-sustaining. However, without a suitable digital marketing approach, you will stand to lose out on online value propositions, online market shares, valuable resources, time as well as money. Before you begin tracking your metrics, though, you need to determine what your targets are. In any marketing campaign, the first move is always to identify what your targets are. All of these goals have to be ethical, easy to achieve, have a timeline, unique to the company, and comply with the needs of the moment. Setting specific marketing objectives keeps you focused on your goals. Objectives can be categorized by measurability indexes, relevancy, and time. If you're just starting out in your digital journey, these are the most important metrics that you should be tracking for your campaigns (you can always add more metrics later on when your budget and your team has grown bigger):

- **Your Customer Conversion Rates -** Since the rate of returning visitors to a site is essential to maintain the popularity and effectiveness of your campaigns, you need to know how many customers you have successfully converted from your marketing campaigns. Your customer conversion rates would be the element you need to help you define your targets for your online purchases, web visits, contact forms, newsletter subscriptions, and times spent on a page. It could also be used to track other user interactions on the site and user interactions on social media. As for measuring website traffic and referral sources to check which strategies work efficiently, you would go through Google Analytics for those numbers.

- **Cost-Per-Measure** - Otherwise known by its acronym *CPM.* Your CPM will tell you how much it will cost for you to reach a thousand users, for example, and it will vary depending on the platform that you use.

- **Cost-Per-View** - Your Cost-Per-View (CPV) is an important one to keep an eye on, especially if you're running video campaigns. If you're relying on campaigns where you need to optimize your video viewership, this is the metric that will tell you if you're on the right track.

- **Click-Through-Rate (CTR)** - This metric is mainly for website traffic campaigns. These numbers would reflect how many people clicked on your actual ad.

- **Cost-Per-Click (CPC)** - This would be the metric that you turn to if you were doing a website traffic related campaign.

- **Cost-Per-Action (CPA)** - This would be the cost involved for your audience to take action. An action could be several different things. For example, an action could be how much it would cost to get someone to submit a lead on your website, or the cost per store visit, for example. It could also be tied to your website metrics. For example, the cost involved for a customer to spend four minutes on your website. This lower funnel metric will reflect the impact that your advertising efforts are having on your customers. If you want to know whether your message is getting through to them, this would be the metric to focus on.

- **Video Completion Rate (VCR)** - This would be where you track the number of viewers you started and completed your video all the way to the end. This metric is going to tell you whether your digital storytelling was as successful as you hoped it would be. This might not be your main KPI though, since it would depend on what your objectives for the campaign are.

- **Return on Advertising Spend (ROAS)** - These numbers will reflect how much money you have put into your ads versus how much money you have gained back from that investment. For example, if you were running a paid social media campaign or search campaign and you invested $10,000 and gained $20,000 back, that would mean that your ROAS was successful. If you wanted to look at the efficiency of your investment, this would be your ROAS, since you want to be sure that you're putting your money where you're getting the most return.

Conclusion

Thank you for making it through to the end of *Digital Strategy*, let's hope it was informative and able to provide you with all of the tools you need to achieve your goals whatever they may be.

Your business model needs to survive in the digital world, because the digital world is here to stay. If you want to survive, you have to adapt to the demands of this landscape, and the having a sound digital strategy with all the right tools for success is *the best* way to begin.

The digital world is evolving quickly, and your business needs to be *even quicker* if you don't want to be left behind. The good news here is that you now have all the tools you need to set you off on the path to success. All that is left is to implement these seven steps and begin crafting the perfect digital strategy for your business. Think of this guide as your Launchpad, and if all the tools here are used in the right way, it can take your business to great heights.

Book 2: Social Media Marketing

7 Easy Steps to Master Social Media Advertising, Influencer Marketing & Platform Audience Growth

Santino Spencer

Introduction

Welcome to *Social Media Marketing;* whether you are trying to run a business or just up your social media marketing game, you have made a great choice. The seven steps shared within *Social Media Marketing* will provide great value to enhance your success. Every business, regardless of size, has to have some type of strategy for social media marketing. Simply going about social media marking without a plan can be very costly and honestly might even hurt your brand.

Social media has become the fastest moving industry in the world. Businesses can grow faster, find new customers quicker, grow their wealth and knowledge by reaching out to people from all over the world. This is something that was not possible several decades ago when the only form of marketing accessible to most businesses was print, radio, and television advertising. Your reach was restricted based on your budget, and you had no control over how many times your target audience would listen or see the content you are putting out there. Well, not anymore.

One of social media's most powerful features is the way it can connect people from all over the world in a matter of seconds. It doesn't matter where you are located, as long as you have a working internet connection and some device to view content on, you're connected. For businesses, this has been an *incredible* advantage. Imagine the business potential when you can now reach millions of customers worldwide?

Social media has changed the world of marketing forever. For example, your business can go live in a matter of seconds to people across the world. Your product launch, when it is done as live broadcast, it is instantly shown to customers from every country imaginable. You get to share the amazing things that happen in your company with your loyal customers and build relationships with them in a way that you never could before social media came along.

This platform has forced businesses to become more creative, innovative, and more attentive to what the customers want in order to keep the content fresh, relevant, and appealing to the target audience. Social media has also become a hotbed of research, and this is where *your business* begins to transform your marketing strategies. The seven-step approach in the next few chapters will be your guide to marketing your business on this social, digital space like a winner. Let's get started.

Chapter 1: Step 1 – Understand Why Your Business Needs It

Social media is the king of the marketing world. There is no one out there who *has not* heard of social media and what an incredible force it can be. Companies have gone from being unknown to a household name through the sheer power of social media marketing alone. Since it was created, social media has changed and revolutionized the internet. Despite the pros and cons, there is no denying that every single business out there is going to need social media marketing to remain competitive.

More importantly, you need social media if you want to stay in business. Customers these days *expect* you to have some kind of social media presence before they can even think about taking you seriously. Let's put it this way, if your competitor has a social media presence and you don't, they are going to go to your competitors, no matter how fabulous your product may be.

What Is It?

Customers don't want to be handed flyers or brochures with your sales pitch on it anymore. Customers today are only going to be interested in what you have to sell if you find a way to engage with them in an interesting and relevant way. That is where social media comes into play. Social media marketing is basically marketing that is done on social media platforms. You will be using platforms like Facebook, Instagram, or Twitter, for example, to announce new product launches, introduce new services, talk about your latest line, and a whole lot more. Yes, it is that simple.

To be honest, it is not that far different from the old marketing methods that businesses and companies have been employing even before social media was a thing. It is still marketing, except this time, all the tools and techniques of marketing have been modified to accommodate social media platforms. You're marketing your products on social media instead of print, television, and radio this time.

Social media marketing is an approach that businesses can utilize to interact with their customers and potential customers in the most natural way possible. This can easily be done on the bigger, more popular platforms like Facebook and Twitter, and it can also be done on smaller niche sites that are built around communities. Think of social media as a town hall, where every customer comes together to share stories, ideas, thoughts, opinions, and feedback about a product or service. To touch base with new prospective customers that may be coming through your pipeline and convert them into loyal, paying customers, you need social media platforms to help you achieve that goal.

As for your customers, social media platforms are not marketing machines but social networks. When you start embarking on developing your social media marketing strategy, you may be up against a few challenges. Plenty of companies to in hard and start hard selling to their consumers, which inundates their followers with discount offer codes and new product announcement, even before consumers could even warm up to the brand. When their accounts do not bring the traffic they want, these brands assume that these networks aren't a good fit for them or social media isn't the place to spend their efforts on.

Why Your Business Needs It

There are several reasons why your business needs social media marketing, and these are some of the reasons why you should be utilizing this form of communication as soon as possible:

- *Your Marketing Costs Go Down* - This is probably one of the things businesses love most about social media platforms is the ability to reduce their marketing cost. Yes, it is going to reduce your marketing costs by *a lot*. Compared to traditional marketing methods like print advertising, television, billboards, magazines, or radio channels, marketing on social media is remarkably more affordable.

Don't forget that social media channels itself are *free,* and it does not cost anything to create a free social media account for your business to get the ball rolling.

- ***It Is the Best Way to Showcase Your Brand*** - Social media marketing is by far the best way to showcase your brand these days. In fact, it has become the number one way for a business to increase its brand recognition without having to spend a ton of money on traditional advertising methods. Social media marketing gives your business the opportunity to boost your reputation through your website, search engine optimization, email marketing, and more.

It is an opportunity to drive sales and build relationships with your customers by interacting with them on a one-to-one level, something that was not possible before with traditional forms of marketing. What is even better is that you get to communicate with your customers through your social media pages for *free.* It costs you nothing to respond to their comments, chat messages, and queries. Each time you do that, you're building a connection with your customers, and in the business world, this form of communication and interaction is priceless.

- ***You're Developing a Loyal Following and Community*** - By creating these relationships with your customers, you are indirectly building a loyal community among them as you do this. People have always enjoyed being a part of something. People enjoy being part of a group, a crowd, a club, something that makes them feel a sense of belonging and acceptance. Today, businesses have the opportunity to create such a community among the people through social media marketing. Your customers will enjoy being associated with a brand that is actively building a lively community online, especially if they get to interact with other like-minded customers for some honest feedback and opinions about your products and services.

Customers want value for money these days, and reviews online alone are not going to cut it. They want recommendations and suggestions straight from the horse's mouth, and in this case, the proverbial horse would be the other customers. By building a community like this, you are helping your customers establish an emotional connection with your brand, and if you trigger the right emotions, you make them customers for life. This is the kind of relationship that is essential for your long-term success.

- **Better Customer Service** - A successful business is no longer about just the purchase and sale of products anymore. Customers expect more than merely purchasing your products and letting that be the end of the story. Oh no, these days, customers want to share their feedback and thoughts about your products, and social media is the best channel for them to do this. Not only does social media allow your customers to communicate directly with your company, but they can also communicate with each other. Word of mouth is one of the best forms of free marketing you can get your hands on.

There is nothing like a good word or recommendation from a source to have other customers flocking to your business, eager to get their hands on your products too. Plus, being able to communicate directly with your business helps to enhance your brand's trustworthiness while simultaneously improving your customer service. With the old way of marketing, a business was nothing more than a cold, distant entity to the customer. Today, businesses and customers can interact instantaneously with each other as old friends would.

- *It Increases Your Digital Exposure* - By actively interacting on your social media channels, you are significantly increasing your online presence. A customer will remember and prefer a business that is actively responding to their messages or comments within a reasonable timeframe. One of the reasons why social media is an incredible platform for maximizing your brand's exposure is because of its worldwide presence. It is accessible to everyone in the world with an internet connection and at least a smartphone.

Social media accounts are free to set up, and this means that every single one of your customers is ninety-nine percent very likely to own at least one type of social media account. In fact, a lot of shopping these days happens on social media accounts, not just websites alone anymore. The massive number of daily users and its incredible content-sharing capabilities means news about your business will spread in a matter of seconds. Five minutes from now, your brand name could be introduced to someone halfway across the world from you, all through the incredible power of social media.

- *It Helps to Boost Your Traffic and Search Engine Rating* - Social media platforms are major lead generators. They bring a consistent stream of high-volume traffic to your website and maximize your search engine optimization (SEO). Search engines can significantly reflect your social media content with the right keywords. This is potential that no business can afford to miss out on.

- *It Expands Your Sales and Reaches New Groups of Audiences Quickly* - Nothing else can generate new sales and reach new customers as quickly as social media can, once again, thanks to its incredible worldwide reach. By monitoring and listening to the conversations that are happening on your social media pages *from your customers,* this is an opportunity to address their needs *specifically.* Businesses never had this opportunity before social media came along. Back then, you could only guess the specifics of what your customer wanted based on surveys or questionnaires. By addressing what they need, it expands your sales and increases your customer base.

Traditional forms of marketing, while still being used today, are slowly on their way out. It is the age of the internet where everything is online, everything is immediate, and almost everyone is accessible with just a few clicks of the mouse. Social media platforms are the easiest and most convenient way for people to keep in touch even if they may be halfway across the globe. Businesses realize that today's consumer is shifting away from those old advertising forms. Today, the attention is on social media platforms, and this is where you need to be. You need to go where your customers are.

Chapter 2: Step 2 - Market Research Done Right

Did you know that social media marketing could be used for in-depth information into your market research process? For any business, it is important that your product or service is all about the consumer. Everything that you do should be all about your customers. This is where market research plays a vital role in keeping up with what your customers want and expect from your business. Since they are paying money for your products and services, they will be expecting you to provide what they are looking for.

What Is Social Media Market Research?

This is the type of research that acknowledges your branding and the way that your business is reaching your target audience. In other words, it tells you whether your marketing campaigns are effectively progressing the way that you hoped it would. It gives you insight into the marketing methods you have been using on each of your social media platforms in the past, present, and future. The research conducted will point out whether your efforts have been effective in achieving your business goals.

The Benefits of Market Research

For the answers to your *who, what, where, when, why*, and *how* questions, you need market research. Market research is a valuable tool that has long been used by businesses to better understand the needs and demands of their target audience base. Thanks to social media, however, not only do businesses get to research what their customers are up to, they also get to research what their competitors are doing too. The kiss of death for any business is to assume that they know that the customers' needs are, or to assume that they should just go ahead and build a business first, and the marketing will take care of bringing the customers in. That is just a warrant for failure.

In the business world, every single decision that is being made in the interest of the business needs to have a foundation on concrete and undeniable research proof behind it, even for campaigns that are being run on social media. Besides giving you intel into the minds of your customers, market research is beneficial for the following reasons:

- It keeps you focused on your business plan and ensures that you are always looking ahead at what the next step should be.

- It reminds you to listen to your target audience whenever you're thinking about coming up with a new product or service line. Give the people what they want, and they will keep coming back to you for more.

- It tells you what problems you need to solve for your customers and helps you create the right product to get the job done.

- Market research helps you identify what your business opportunities are. When you know what the customer wants, you can start strategizing about what needs to be done to meet those needs and demands. This puts you in a unique position to take advantage of opportunities your competition may not have had a chance to yet.

- Market research ensures that you stay relevant, and in doing so, you keep your business relevant. Staying relevant and keeping your customers loyal is about being able to meet and fulfill the needs that they have. If they don't get it from your business, they will get it from your competitors, and there is no amount of marketing you can do that will keep your customers with you if you are not meeting their needs.

- It cuts down on the risks and losses you experience per campaign. Research supplies your business with the necessary and vital information you need to decide on what the right approach or the next step should be. This keeps the risks to a minimum because you will not be stumbling blindly forward hoping that their plan is going to work. With your research in hand, you will know for a fact what the right move should be because they have the research on hand to back it up.

- Market research helps to point out what your current and potential business issues are. As a business, you need to pay close attention to the feedback that is being received by your market research audience because oftentimes, they will be able to shed light on an area that may not even be seen as a problem for the company but raises issues with its target market.

- Market research makes your customers feel happy because it tells them that your business is listening to their concerns. When customers feel that they are being heard and that a business is taking the time to find out what they want, there is a higher chance that they will remain loyal to the businesses.

Primary and Secondary Market Research

Market research is divided into two categories, primary and secondary. Primary market research is the most important type of research for your business. It is research that is done in real-time, and it is research that you are doing yourself. Primary research is where you start from scratch with information that does not exist yet. Not until you create it. You are conducting this research to find the information and data that you need. Traditionally, primary market research was a costly affair. It was conducted through focus groups, interviews, and surveys. In this aspect, social media has been a complete game-changer. With social media, the valuable primary market research information you need can be collected *for free.* You can conduct polls on social media for free, conduct interviews with special guests on your live streams and make a note of the questions your customers ask, and much more.

Your secondary research is information that already exists, like your customers' interests based on their profiles, the types of questions they've already asked you. All you have to do is analyze the existing research to see how you can use it to your advantage. Examples of where you would go for secondary research include case studies conducted by your competitors if the information is available online, tuning in to your competitor's live streams, or analyzing the results from previous campaigns and surveys you have conducted in the past.

Both primary and secondary research have their benefits, but primary research has a more personalized factor to it. Plus, primary research gives you access to the latest information that is relevant to your customers. Today, you can run polls on your Facebook and Instagram stories. It only takes mere seconds for your customers to quickly tap on the answers they prefer, and there you go. You have instant answers to your questions. The authenticity of the information you gather from this approach is extraordinary. For example, by showcasing different products across your Instagram or Facebook

Stories feature throughout the week, you might be surprised to learn which are your most popular and least popular products. With access to information like this, you can instantly revise your key selling points and campaign focus as you go.

Social Media Channels That Are Good for Research

The different social media channels can provide insight and contribute to your research in various ways:

- *Facebook Groups* - Join a Facebook group that your target audience is part of and start participating in the discussions. If you prefer to be a passive observer that just watches and reads what people are talking about in these groups, you can do that too. Facebook Groups also give you the option of using question polls as part of your research. You can type out a question (a primary market research method) and get the answers that you are looking for to help you develop your next content or product.

- *Twitter* - Twitter allows you the option of creating lists. You can put your target audience on these lists, either on one list or a couple of different lists, depending on what your research objective is. Having these lists makes it easier for you to scroll through to find out what your customer interests are, what content they are tweeting about, the hashtags they use, and more. You also have the option of creating a competitor's list, where you put your competitors on a specific list to go through to research the type of content they are putting out, the hashtags they use, and the content they are tweeting about too.

- *YouTube* - On YouTube, you can source for content that is similar to yours and go through the comments section to see the types of questions that are being asked. You can find out a surprising amount of information about your target audience this way, like the types of problems they have and the answers they are looking for. By going through these comments, it can help you develop content that *they* are interested in, enticing them to your page instead of your competitor's.

- *Live Streams* - These Live Streams are available on most social media platforms. It notifies your followers when your business is broadcasting live. For example, once you start your live stream, your customers that follow your account are going to get a notification on their phone saying you've gone live, and they'll quickly tune in to your content. This is a fantastic approach to conducting some immediate market research by conducting a question and answer session.

- *Surveys* - This one is a traditional marketing tactic that has existed even before the days of the internet. Surveys are a primary market research method that is still being used today because it still has a purpose. Websites like Survey Monkey make it easy to quickly create a free survey that you can quickly send to your customers. You can post your survey on your Facebook page, website, Instagram, and other social media platforms that you prefer.

Chapter 3: Step 3 - How to Market on Facebook

You could be just starting out with your Facebook marketing tactics, or you could be a seasoned marketer. Either way, every business is always on the lookout for ways to improve their marketing strategies so they can market on Facebook like a winner. Whether your goal is to boost your following or engagement rate, no matter what your goals are, you need to have the right strategies in order to make it work. Facebook is a crowded space with millions of contents being shared daily by individual users and businesses alike. The only way to be a winner in this platform is to stand out with the right marketing tactics.

Your Content Is Where the Magic Happens

Facebook is your platform, but your content is where the magic happens. If you want your content to stand out, it has to be incredible. There is a lot of content that gets posted on Facebook daily, and this means it is going to take something remarkable to make an impression on your target audience. Your content is not the only one they will be exposed to on a daily basis, and it is important that you make a strong enough first impression with every piece of content you post if you want your business to stay at the forefront of their minds.

As businesses, brands, and marketers, quality content should be your focal point with everything that you post. Before you hit the publish button, the question you need to ask yourself is, *"is my content worth noticing?"*. A good tip to keep in mind when you are trying to create and curate your quality content is to focus on a niche. Instead of trying to target the billions of users on Facebook, even though it is tempting to try and bring in as many customers as possible, you will be much better off targeting a subset of users instead. This makes it much easier to produce useful content that is equally entertaining to this niche group. When you know who you are targeting and what they want to see from you, it makes it easier to come up with quality content that matters.

Another way to create quality content is to focus on what your goals are. For example, if your goal was to drive traffic to your website, then you would focus on content that is specifically designed to encourage your target audience to flock to your website. Having goals in mind gives you a purpose, and with that purpose, you can begin creating the type of content you need to meet those goals. For effective marketing, ninety percent of your time should be spent on creating content, while the other ten percent of that time is focused on posting the content. Avoid the mistake of getting too caught up with trying to post as much as possible in the hopes of staying relevant on your audience's page. They would much rather see you post once a day but posting something that is useful to them, instead of posting frivolous content five times a day. It is not the quantity; it is the quality that matters.

Focus on Creating Video Content

The majority of your audience these days is going to be more interested in video content over everything else. Mark Zuckerberg himself once said that videos are the future of social media. Facebook's algorithm even focuses on placing video content at the top of the newsfeed. If you were to analyze your statistics over the course of a few months, you would probably notice that your video content is going to see the most successful compared to any other type of content you produce. You don't need a lot of resources or a big team to create quality video content. In fact, it is much easier than you think, and quality content begins by keeping these few tips in mind when you're making your videos:

- Avoid being too "sales-y" with your videos. Videos should be used as a brand awareness tool, not a sales pitch.

- Keep your videos to a maximum of two minutes. The top-performing videos on this platform are usually between sixty and ninety seconds long.

- Keep the captions in your videos between fifty to a hundred characters. Your audience does not have time to read long and lengthy captions. Ideally, you want your captions to capture the gist of the overall message.

Another important factor to keep in mind is that more than ninety percent of your audience is most likely going to be viewing your content on their mobile phones. This means that your target audience would be scrolling through their feed quickly, and therefore, they don't have time for long and lengthy content. Users have very short attention spans, and they will easily be distracted by other things going on around them. To win them over, you need to keep your videos short, to the point, and put your *best content* at the *front of your video.* You only have seconds to intrigue your audience enough to make them watch your video all the way through, and you need to make those first few seconds count.

Why You Should Be Sharing Curated Content

Creating new content is time-consuming, and despite your best efforts, there may be times when you are so busy running the business that you simply don't have time to create new content. To supplement this, what you could do is share curated content. Share content from another top, reputable source that is from within your industry. You don't have to worry about replacing the content strategy of your own business when you do this. Sharing curated content is merely a supplement to help you maintain a consistent voice and posting on social media.

There is a benefit to sharing curated content from other sources too. If all you do is post content about your business all the time, people are going to start tuning you out after a while because it is all the same thing. There is nothing that keeps it fresh, interesting, and exciting on your page. By sharing curated content from others, you are strengthening your position as an industry leader, showing your audience your vast knowledge on the subject. Another benefit of doing this is that you get to build relationships with the people whose content you are sharing.

Repurpose Your Top Performing Content

Do you have content that has performed well in the past? Why not share it again? Not all your users are going to see every piece of content that you post. There is no harm in re-sharing old content. The one rule of thumb to keep in mind when you do this is to wait at least a month before you re-share any piece of content. Allow some time to pass before you put this post up again. Ideally, you would want a never-ending supply of fresh, new, and great content you can post to your Facebook page. However, since this is not always the case, your next best option would be to re-share what already proved to be popular in the past.

Focus on Your "Pages to Watch"

This is one of the most powerful tools you can use to create great social media content. You will get access to your "Pages to Watch" feature once you have seventy-five likes or more on your page. With this feature, you get to watch up to a hundred pages. It could be your competitors, inspirational pages that you love, and any sort of page you would like. Once you have a list of pages that you can find inspiration from daily, you can use this for ideas to guide your own Facebook strategy. The top three ways to use this "Pages to Watch" feature include the following:

- You could use this as a guide to set goals and benchmarks for your own brand. For example, you could use it to set audience engagement or growth goals.

- You could use this feature to curate content. Facebook even ranks the most popular type of content first, literally making your job easier by telling you what content has proven to be the most popular on other similar pages.

Listen to Your People

A lot of businesses will say that they struggle to come up with content. Why do they struggle? Because they are not listening to their audience. One of the most important foundations of any marketing strategy, whether it is social media or conventional marketing techniques, is listening to your target market. If you listen to your people, they will *tell you what they want to see and hear from you.* You don't have to spend hours brainstorming new and fresh ideas, all you have to do is learn to listen. Once you have gathered these details, you can create content that is tailored to their interests and needs and spark conversations that lead to sales.

Chapter 4: Step 4 - How to Market on Instagram

If you want your Instagram following to grow, it is important to have a strategy that works. This rule of thumb can be applied to all your social media platforms, truth be told. Instagram is a platform that is focused heavily on visual content. It is less about the captions and more about the captivating images. Just like Facebook, this platform is also one of the stronger social media tools for marketing and brand building, although it uses a different approach. Instagram's core strengths lie in its vivid imagery gallery, and for businesses like retailers, clothing companies, jewelry companies, travel companies, and any business that relies heavily on presenting itself through images, this is an excellent social media platform to do so. Instagram should be treated as a marketing tool and part of your entire overall marketing strategy. It may be a powerful social media platform, but it is not a standalone method for building your business.

Instagram has the potential to generate hundreds of new customers each month, but only if you're going about it the right way.

You Need to Have a Plan

You need to have a plan because it is going to guide your efforts and point you in the right direction. Your outcome is going to be a lot more fruitful if you have a good sense of where you should be going.

When you are developing your marketing strategy, spend some time thinking about what your primary goal with your Instagram account is. Avoid simply snapping and recording anything just for the sake of appearing active on your social media account. In order to post successfully captivating images and videos, the content needs to tell a story. All images and videos that get posted on Instagram will be a reflection of your business, and therefore, you want each content you put out there to link back to your overall business goals.

Here's a hint you might not have thought about. Your goal *should not be* trying to grow your following. That's right, you need to think bigger than that. Your goals should be along the lines of getting more traffic to your website, building your email list, boosting the sales of your products or service, and not about how many likes you can get on a picture you posted this morning or how many followers you've gained. Of course, it is always good news to see your numbers growing in terms of followers. It means your business is getting noticed, but there is a lot more potential to be tapped into with Instagram. Think bigger with your goals and use Instagram to help you reach those goals.

Create Shareable Content

What most businesses would do is create content that is focused entirely on their business. Of course, that is what you should be doing, isn't it? Are you only creating content that is all about you? Well, not necessarily. What you should do instead is create content that other people can share.

Identify Who Your Target Market Is

Not sure who your target market is? Then you have work to do. Like all social media platforms, you need to know who your target market is because it is an important element of your business. Your customers are the lifeline of your business, and if you target the wrong groups, you're wasting all the time, energy, and resources you committed to marketing on Instagram. Since Instagram can be a rather time-consuming platform, you want to make sure that everything you do on this platform has a purpose.

Since Instagram is limited to visual postings, you need to think about how to take your connection with your followers a step further by reaching out even more. One example of how you do this is to provide a link in your description section that directs back to your company's website or landing page. A lot of websites these days have a call to action feature the minute a user lands on their site by either asking them to simply subscribe to a newsletter.

This is why it is important to identify your target market. When a user subscribes, companies get access to the user's email, and this will then allow them to send updates and reach out to the users directly into their inbox. When posting images and videos on your social media platform, prompt the audience with a call to action by redirecting them back to the link on your bio. Your target market will be the group of people who will benefit the most from your offerings. This is going to be different for every business, depending on what your brand and your business represent. Identify as much information as you can about your target market, and this will allow you to create content that is specifically relevant to what they want to see from you.

Your Account Needs to Be Visible

Avoid the mistake of making your account private. You would be surprised at how often this little detail gets overlooked. Privatizing your personal account is fine, but your business account should remain as accessible as possible. Your target customers and audience base need to be able to locate you on Instagram, and it won't help if your account is private, and they have no access to the content your business offers unless they follow your account. Your target customers don't want to feel like they are being forced into joining or following your business, they want to be able to choose it. Make your content visible and easy to find on the social media platform, and make it likable enough that the audience wants to keep tabs with what you're doing by being a follower.

Use Your Hashtags Sparingly

Hashtags are the most popular on Instagram, although Twitter and Facebook do incorporate the use of hashtags on their platforms as well, it was never still quite as popular as it is on Instagram. In fact, one of the primary ways of discovering a new person, product, group, or business on Instagram is through hashtags. Hashtags are one of Instagram's main marketing strengths because not only does it make it easy for users to discover a business, businesses also find it easier to track potential consumers. Avoid being tempted to bombard your post with every single hashtag that pops into your mind. Focus on the ones that link back to your business.

Customers and audiences who are on the lookout for something specific will have a better chance of locating your content when the right hashtags have been put into place. The key tip here is to ensure everything posted, from content to texts and hashtags are in unison and complement one another. Before posting any content, it's recommended that you look at the trending hashtags of the day and narrow down the ones that are related to your business and content. If it's relevant then go ahead and use it, but if it's not, then ditch it.

Create Content That Is Strategic

Once you deeply understand who your target audience is, creating content that matters becomes a whole lot easier. Every photo, video, and the caption that you take should speak directly to your customer.

Be clear about what your business is offering. Your content should offer a solution and provide value to your customers and your followers. If your target customers and the audience are not sure of what your business is selling, you lose the potential to gain new customers because they will lose interest.

People like to know what they're dealing with, and businesses who don't have a strong, clear presence and message are going to be on the losing end. When you aim to create content specifically for a demographic, you are going to naturally attract them to your Instagram feed. They will decide that they *want* to follow you because they can relate to everything that you post. When your content makes them feel like you are speaking directly to them, it can convert them into loyal, paying customers. If you create random content, you might end up attracting a mix of people and get a higher number of followers, but they might not take the action that you want.

Engage with Your Target Audience Regularly

To consistently attract the right kind of audience who will take the action you want, you need to engage with your target market regularly.

Create Vertical Video Content

Video marketing is a must for anyone running a business. Many successful businesses acknowledge that videos are crucial and a necessary tool as part of their overall marketing strategy. To make the best impact possible on your viewers, you need to fully utilize the video marketing capabilities on Instagram. Thanks to videos being primarily shot on smartphones these days by users themselves, the vertical video trend has increased in popularity so much that they outperform the horizontal videos in every way.

It's a mobile world out there. Users are on their mobiles more than their desktops these days. At the end of each video, don't forget to include a call to action that will ask and remind your audience to take a specific action. A call to action encourages your audience to take the next step toward your primary goal and move along in your marketing funnel.

Chapter 5: Step 5 - How to Market on YouTube

What videos should you make for your business's YouTube channel? How will your target audience find you? Where do you even begin making content that is going to get your business noticed and skyrocket your marketing goals? It all comes down to three key things:

- Your strategy
- How to set up your channel
- How to secure your first few subscribers

Your YouTube Marketing Strategy

YouTube is one of the best platforms for business to engage with current and prospective customers because not only is YouTube a cost-effective marketing platform, but it has a much bigger reach than any other video dissemination platform out there. With more than a billion users to date and counting, this is one marketing opportunity you cannot afford to pass up.

YouTube is such an easy marketing tool for businesses to make use of because of how easy it is to share videos online. YouTube videos are also easily shareable on other social media platforms, which makes it easy for businesses to promote the content many times over on their other social media accounts like Facebook and Twitter, doubling or tripling a YouTube video's reach just like that.

Now, the number one mistake that a lot of companies make with YouTube is not creating content *and thumbnails* that are interesting enough. Yes, your thumbnails have to be equally attractive because that is the first thing your customers will look at. Would you click on a thumbnail that didn't intrigue you? Probably not, and your customers will think the same. Many businesses get so caught up in creating interesting content of value that they forget they need to make their thumbnails attractive on their profile too.

The first step in creating a marketing strategy on YouTube is just like any other social platform, and it begins with defining your goals. With YouTube, you want to write down specific targets that you want to achieve, such as clicks and traffic, engagement as well as reach and subscriber numbers. If you want your audience to watch your videos, then you need to make videos that they *want to watch*. Otherwise, they are not going to watch, it is as simple as that.

The questions to ask when you're thinking about crafting your YouTube strategy for your video content are:

- What value can I add to my videos that the customer would appreciate?
- What is my target audience interested in?

- What videos would my target audience be willing to watch willingly without them feeling like they are being forced into it?

Value is added to your videos by *teaching* your audience something new, something useful, and something that will benefit them. You also add value by entertaining them through your videos and triggering emotions. How-to videos are among the high-performing videos on YouTube because they provide plenty of value to users. Since YouTube is the second most used search engine, people go to YouTube because they want to see something done or learn how to make something or cook something or build something.

How-To videos are great for plenty of business, no matter what industry you are in. If you are using this format, you need to look at what aspect of your business can be turned into a "How-To." For instance, you sell car engine oil. You can do a tutorial on how to use this oil, how to change your car engine oil, and the benefits of good oil. Look upon the internet for blog posts for materials you can use to create your video. Make this video edutainment.

Setting Up Your Channel

There are two types of channels you can set up. The first type of channel is where you have your profile as your main channel. The second channel is your brand channel. You need to set up a brand channel to gain access to the features you need to share with your employees and other people in the company who are also working on maintaining your channel. Every channel needs to have the following design elements:

- Your profile picture
- Your channel image
- Custom thumbnails (remember, your thumbnails need to be just as interesting and engaging as your videos)

An important note to keep in mind is that you need the elements on your channel to be consistent. Your brand needs to be represented in all your content. There are several ways you can optimize your channel too, and some of these elements are within your control, and some are not. Keywords that you use and how you use them are completely in your control, however, elements like how many people subscribe immediately after viewing your videos are not exactly things that you can control or have power on.

Going back to the importance of thumbnails, the right kind of thumbnail will attract a reader to click on it, making your video trend as well as make your channel recognizable. Just like the title, your thumbnail should be relevant to the content as well as correspond with your video title. Attractive thumbnails result in higher clicks. You should also include short descriptions in your thumbnail so viewers can understand what your video is all about. You want to immediately catch the interest of your viewers by telling them a quick story just by your thumbnails and your title. Not only should these elements tell viewers what your video is all about, but it should also make them curious enough to want to watch your videos. Make a template or style guide for your thumbnails to maintain consistency here too.

Getting Your First Few Subscribers

Getting your first few subscribers is usually one of the biggest challenges that a company would face on YouTube. In such a vast space with millions of videos all vying for your attention, how do you get your content to stand out enough that people *want* to subscribe to your channel? This is even more important if you're already a big and established brand since it can look rather unprofessional if you only have a few subscribers. Well, the first step is easy, and that is to leverage your existing social media accounts. Use your Facebook, Twitter, Instagram, newsletters, and blogs to get the ball rolling. Try to send the existing audience there over to your channel.

Another thing that you could do is to work together with other channels and other YouTubers. Video collaboration is popular among YouTubers, and it is a great way to gain a new audience base as well as increase your subscriber base. It is a win-win situation for both YouTubers as well as the target audience since the audience will get to see their favorite YouTubers together working on something or creating something. Working with influencers is not an uncommon strategy. In fact, many brands are starting to leverage the potential that working with influencers can bring to their business. Collaboration has so many obvious advantages, so long as you do it with the right people and brands.

Social media influencers are powerful. They can drive traffic to your Facebook page overnight by simply putting in a few good words and a well-crafted video upload. Especially if they're demonstrating how your product is being used. According to Forbes, what they revealed was that MuseFind, an influencer marketing platform, found that audiences were ninety-two percent more likely to trust the word of a social media influencer compared with an ad. Sometimes, these brands or people don't necessarily have to be in your industry, and you could try looking for complimenting brands and influencers to work with as this will grow your audience exponentially. The potential for content creation here is enormous.

Collaboration is one of the very best ways to add some entertainment value to your content. Apart from connecting with your audience, you can also use social media to connect with experts, influencers, and industry leaders, thus enhancing your status as an authoritative expert and credible source of information for your industry. The huge rise of social media platforms has also given birth to a new trend of social media influencers. These influencers use their popularity to market products and services to generate income.

An influencer is an individual who has huge popularity or followers that listen or emulate them. They collaborate with marketers to promote products, services, and even events to their followers. This has pushed many ad agencies to increase their budget on social media influencer marketing to catch this trend. A social media influencer is described as someone who has a lot of followers online. They are generally an expert or an authority on a particular subject, although celebrities fall under the influencer category too because of the immense pull they have. What an influencer buys, wears, or says can influence the decision of their followers. Over time, you are more than just a brand, you are part of a community. This change of perception also leads towards higher ROI, which means you'll also get plenty of exposure. With higher ROI, you get more exposure, and with more exposure, comes leads and new leads turn into followers. These followers turn into potential customers.

Chapter 6: Step 6 - Focusing on the Right Niche Market

Everyday there are thousands of people are searching for various products and services to buy. They might need these products and services to help fulfil a need or want that they have. Your job as a business is to find the right people who are looking for the kind of products and services that you offer. Those specific people are your niche market group.

What Is a Niche Market?

A niche market is a group of people who are looking for a specific product. For example, if your business was selling health supplements, your niche market would be that specific group of people who were looking for the kind of health supplements you provide. Your niche market would depend on the kind of products and services that you sell. Another example would be if you were in the business of selling baby products. Baby products can be divided into a few categories, like baby shoes, clothing, food, bath products, and more. Baby shoes would be one of the niche market consumers you would target.

If you want to grow your business and achieve all your goal milestones, then you need to be focused on marketing to your niche audience. The logic behind this is simple, if your audience is far too broad and general, a lot of your efforts could be wasted on targeting those who are not even remotely interested in your content. The narrower and more niche your target audience is, the better your return on investment will be. This will help you write better content, more compelling posts, and more engaging information. These benefits, however, extend beyond marketing. You create brand loyalty and credibility, it helps you identify customer pain points, create a loyal following, refine product strategies, and improve sales conversions. To be effective with your marketing strategy, you need to aim for where it matters the most. This strategy will end up saving you a lot of time, money, and effort in the long run.

How Do You Find Your Niche Market?

It would depend once again on the kind of products or services you sell. The first thing you need to do is to find a focus. Niche marketing is all about focus. It is a focus on selling and advertising your strategies towards a targeted portion of the market. You do not market to everyone who could benefit from your product or service. Instead, you niche market your products to specific people, focusing exclusively on a group of people or a demographic section of likely customers that would most definitely enjoy or benefit from your products. If you are a writer, you could narrow your focus by limiting your writing to children's books. From there, you can narrow your focus even further by focusing only on books for little girls. You could get even more specific by defining the age range you want to target. The more specific you get with your targeting, the more niche your target market becomes.

You could target your audience based on geographic area, lifestyle, occasion, profession, style, culture, activity or habits, behavior, demographic, need, and more. The biggest concern that businesses have when it comes to niche marketing is the fear of losing out on thousands of potential customers. By narrowing your focus like that, you might be concerned that other people are missing out on your products, and therefore, you are missing out on a potential sale. This is a catch twenty-two because the answer is both yes and no. Not every business can be as booming as Amazon is, selling products that cater to practically everyone on the planet. Even if you do want to be like Amazon, Amazon didn't start out that way in the beginning. They had a specific niche they were focusing on too, and they sold books. Over time, they eventually progressed to the Amazon that we know and love today, where they are selling products in almost every category.

When you define a niche for yourself, you enter into a market with potentially less competition. Niche marketing's biggest benefit would be that it allows brands to stand out from the pack and appear unique. This will make sure it resonates better with its already unique and distinct customer section. A brand can employ niche marketing initiatives to stand out and be more valuable rather than blend in, to reach a higher growth potential and ultimately build a better, stronger, and long-lasting relationship with its target market. When you have a shoestring budget, or you're just getting started in the business world, minimal competition is good news, and that is why you should start out by focusing on a niche.

How do you determine what is the best niche market for your business? Through a lot of research, for one thing. There is going to be a lot of research that is going to go into this stage of your business, but it has to be done. You need to research, compare, and evaluate the current market trends and what you have to work with. When researching prices of items for example, look at several platforms instead of focusing on just one. For example, research current trends on Amazon and eBay, but don't make those the only platforms that you are looking at. Broaden your search to include different types of niches. Look at the higher-priced bracket items, and compare that to the lower bracket items. Compare and evaluate the market trends that you are observing on this platform. What is selling well and what isn't. What trends seem to be doing well and why? The more areas of your business that your research covers, the better.

Finding the right niche is also much easier when you aim to answer the following questions. More importantly, this framework is going to help you find a *profitable niche*. These questions are something that every business can use as a framework to find their target audience. The questions to ask as you seek to pinpoint your niche market include:

- ***You Need to Figure Out Who You Would Like to Speak To (Who)*** - Who are you talking to? This question needs to be answered before you come up with any kind of marketing campaign or catch-y tagline. If you don't know who you are talking to specifically, how would you know what you need to say?

- ***What Problem Are You Trying to Solve? (What)*** - What pain point does your business aim to solve with the products and services that you sell? Who are the customers out there with the same kind of problem? The customers who are looking for a product like yours to help them solve this pain point? That will tell you who your niche market is and the group that you should be targeting. There is a good chance that your product or service could solve more than one problem. If that is the case, what you should do as you try to pinpoint your niche in the early stages is to narrow it to one core problem that you want to focus on.

- ***Be Specific About Your Benefits (Why)*** - When crafting out your marketing message for your niche audience, you need to highlight the benefits of your products. Why should your customer be buying from you? How is your product going to change their life for the better? If the benefit of your product is something that is only found within your product, you should highlight this point when marketing to your niche.

- *Brainstorm Who Will Be the Most Interested in Your Products* - Talk to like-minded business friends who could give you some other insight, or perhaps even more ideas, maybe even have a brainstorming session or two with them. Talk to friends and family who are supportive because they too may be able to come up with some pretty good ideas that you could work with. Brainstorming sessions should be done as often as you feel it is necessary. Set a time for it, block out your calendar for a couple of hours to commit to this brainstorming focus entirely on that. Write down everything you know about possible session, and niche options, list them down in order of competition, loyalty, pricing, returns, and more. Compare and contrast which niche is going to give you the best returns, and you may have your answer in front of you on those pieces of paper where you just poured out all your ideas.

- *Have You Tried Looking on Amazon?* - As one of the biggest retailers in the world, Amazon sells just about everything on its platform. Thanks to the presence and reputation it has built for itself over the years, this is now one of the best platforms that you could use at your disposal to find a profitable niche market for your own business. Searching for a potential niche on Amazon is easy. All you would need to do is simply click the "All" tab that is located on the left side of the main search bar, and from there, you will easily find a list of categories which you can select from. Simply find a niche category that grabs your interest, click the "Go" button, and wait for the new page to pop up. On the left side of that page, you will then see the option to select a "sub-niche" category, and by clicking that link, you will be able to view even more specific sub-niches. It's a great platform to source for potential options, and the best part is you will be able to view which products are doing and selling well. Searching for best-selling products is easy. All you would need to do is click on the "Best Sellers" tab from the navigation bar, and there you go.

Chapter 7: Step 7 - Build an Unforgettable Presence

If we strike small talk with a random person, and we find the conversation stimulating and interesting, it will often lead to a full-blown conversation. This is a face-to-face scenario, and more often than not, face-to-face conversations get a little bit more time to convince the other person to listen to you but online communication? Communication on social media? Well, that's another story entirely.

You see, getting someone's attention on social media, or specifically getting your target user's attention on social media is much harder than approaching them and talking to them. Average users only need 8 seconds before they decide the content, they are viewing is not for them. This ultimately means that your conversations on social media not only has to be engaging, it also has to be dynamic and diverse. In short, you need to stand out. You need to give your users a lasting and unforgettable presence.

The Importance of Social Media Presence

Why is it so important to create an unforgettable presence on social media?

Here's why:

- Consumers do not want regurgitated thoughts. They are not looking for flashy promises or empty content.
- Consumers want real value, originality, and excitement.
- They are looking for content that helps them solve their problems.
- They want to make purchasing decisions on what excites them, what helps them solve a problem.
- According to a study done by NewsCred, 62% of millennials say that their loyalty to a brand is directly connected to the quality of the content that the brands they follow produce.

Keep in mind that millennials have been found to spend $200 billion on annual expenditure. This is an extremely important statistic for marketers to keep in mind.

- It's no more about churning out anything just to have something online.
- You need to dedicate content that relates to your business, supports your brand loyalty, and builds your reputation.
- You want to create an unforgettable social media presence so that you are on the top of your consumer's mind the next time they need their problems solved.
- An unforgotten presence ensures continuous growth and effective communication.
- Your consumers are smart and they are not looking for wishy-washy crud or mediocre posts.

In a high-stakes environment where it is harder than ever before to earn attention online, companies must stand out with EPIC content-superb and well-researched material that adds value solves a customer's problem, and has high quality and relevance.

The Benefits of Being Unforgettable

So, what does quality content bring for the marketer and their brand? What are the benefits of being unforgettable on social media?

The effort we put into our content, our look, and the tone of our brand voice and messaging has everything to do with the bottom line-we want profits, and the only way to make profits is to stand out, and the way to stand out is to create epic content.

Being unforgettable on social media brings in more benefits other than increasing our bottom line. Here are some of them:

- More people will talk about you. It'll earn you more shares online, even get you trending.
- You'll have a better reach of your followers- it'll give you a more relevant, exciting, and actionable data to create better content.
- Being unforgettable online lasts longer and is valuable than ordinary content.

- You reach out to a wider pool of people who have stronger brand loyalty and trust in your company.
- Your brand stands out as a thought leader.
- You get to see how adding that extra time and effort into producing. valuable content produced visible results.
- Boring content doesn't produce results, leaving you wondering where you went wrong.

How Do You Make a Lasting Impression?

You probably have an idea of the regular things marketers do to stand out. It is hard to come up with epic content consistently but there are a few things you can do to stay on top and stay unforgettable, and these are the kinds of things that big brands do anyway on a daily basis.

Here they are:

Define Yourself Online-Develop a Consistent Message, Voice, Look and Feel

Consistently sharing and defining your unique message is extremely relevant and valuable to your target audience. You stand out before your brand look & feel is different, but you also stand out because of the language you use to speak to your audience.

Having a consistent message for your brand will enable users to easily identify you from all that clutter and noise. Everything about your online presence needs to be consistent, from your website to your social media channels, your packaging, layout, and even your online banner ads. Consumers need to recognize you instantly.

You do not want your consumers guessing 'who is this brand?' with every message you post out.

Success in being unforgettable leaves no doubt in the consumer's mind- they know who you are, what you care about, and what your values are. It doesn't matter whether they see your logo on a digital banner or on a billboard.

Keep in mind that these values are not only for big businesses. Whether you are a small business owner, entrepreneur, writer, speaker, or budding business, you need to control the narrative in and around your personal brand.

Build a Captivating Social Media Profile

The wonderful thing about social media profiles is that it helps brands present their stories and messages in a fun, creative, and relatable way. These social media platforms also feed data to search engines. Pinpointing your right target audience, who they are, and what they do so you can craft relevant messages is extremely crucial. This makes it easier for your target audience to find you online.

Use every bit of online retail space as best as possible, whether it's on Pinterest or Google+, Instagram, or even the app store. You want to rock your social media profiles with these important points:

- Make sure you tell people who are as simple and as easy as possible. Don't make them guess. A little creativity goes a long way.
- Add links to your blog, website, or any other place you want your consumers to go to.
- Make your profile relatable, accessible, and authentic- these short sentences should be able to tell a story to the search engines as well as to your audience.

Be Authentic

Nobody said you had to be serious all the time- depending on the context. This really depends on how you want to use your brand and leverage on the context and look and feel you're going for. A summary of yourself, your brand, and what you offer has to be authentic so that your audience relates to you.

When you share something authentic, little facts and tidbits about yourself, your past, your struggle, or even your brand, you end up sparking a conversation. People want to know more about you. The fact that you've struggled in your business or had an embarrassing moment happen makes you human, and that appeals to people who have been through a similar situation. Just when your target audience thought you were not relatable, sharing this little info has enabled them to feel a little closer to you and relate to your voice.

Going Organic

Organic growth is the most sustainable of all. Using relevant keywords in an organic way pushes forth a longer, sustainable outcome. You need to dig deep to find out what terms people search for when they look up the niche you are in, the business pool you operate in as well as the product and service you provide. This information should be sewed into your posts, your content, and your keywords.

Google is eager to search and push the story you want to sell so make sure you help Google find you but adding relevant keywords to create a situation that makes it easy to find you and locate you.

Add in Specific Keywords

Keywords are relevant but they do not create the entirety of the solution. Content sells and adding specific keywords that enable you to stand out in your local area, where customers can reach you easily especially if your product or service is a physical one- is extremely crucial.

- ### Add Your Call-to-Action

So, you have your presence set and going on fire, but it will all turn to dust if you do not have a call-to-action to direct your customers to a specific goal you want them to do. Where do you want them to go after viewing your content? What do you want them to click on? Having no place to direct your customers is like getting all dressed up and nowhere to go. Make sure there is a call-to-action on whatever content you are putting out there.

- ***Find Your Uniqueness***

Plenty of successful content creators have found the "one thing" that is their unique identity, that one thing that sells them, that one thing that sets them apart. What's yours? If you haven't figured it out yet, it's ok. As long as you keep working on it, the ideas or the image will become more prevalent. Working with your uniqueness will challenge, excite, and inspire you to continue pushing forth and overcoming whatever challenges there may be.

Conclusion

Thank you for making it through to the end of *Social Media Marketing*, let's hope it was informative and able to provide you with all the tools you need to achieve your goals whatever they may be.

There is no doubt about it, the right social media marketing strategy is going to change your business in ways that you cannot even imagine. There is no better way to build your presence in the digital space than through the immense power of social media. This is one brand awareness and sales tool that you cannot afford to pass up on. Not if you are serious about scaling your business to greater heights, that is.

Social media is a wonderful tool, but it can also prove to be a challenging tool if you don't know where to start. It could also be just as challenging if you are someone who wears multiple hats in your business. Whether your business is big or small, you need social media on your side, that much is clear. Even if you are juggling multiple roles in your business, the key is to identify what aspects of social media you should be focused on to better drive your business. Everything that matters has been covered in this guide. The only thing that is left is for you to get started.

Social media marketing is going to be the very thing that takes your business from mediocre to number one. You want profits, and the only way to make profits is to stand out and the way to stand out is to create epic content, and target the right people with the right strategies. Make a commitment to social media. Make social media marketing a priority for you and your business. Start by planning, create your strategy, create your goals, and identify what success looks like to you. Establish some goals for your social media marketing, and the best thing you can do for your business is to develop goals that align with your social media strategy. Don't forget to be as specific as possible with the details.

Book 3: Business Development

7 Easy Steps to Master Growth Hacking, Lead Generation, Sales Funnels, Traffic & Viral Marketing

Santino Spencer

Introduction

Welcome to *Business Development*. Growth is a core value for anyone doing business; without relationships, strong strategies, brand awareness, and marketplace expansion, businesses are destined to fail. *Business Development* will take you on a guide to expand how you currently think about business and introduce you to some new concepts that are taking the business world by storm; in 7 easy steps.

Defining a business development strategy is an integral part of any organization's growth and success. However, the concept of "business development" is somewhat different for different people. If you ask twelve people what business development is, you will likely end up with twelve different answers. This is largely due to the role of business development changes and grows as the organization grows and changes. The role also will be different based on the age, priority, maturity, and size of the organization.

The easiest way to explain business development is the consistent actions and strategies that contribute to organizational value and growth. Brand awareness, relationship building, and market expansion are all types of strategies that organizations use for business development.

Individuals who work on business development are often assessing the organization's performance and looking for ways to improve organizational growth and prospects. In contrast, those working sales will work directly with customers or clients to close deals. When thinking of business development, you need to think more in a big-picture view or long-term growth perspective.

When it comes to organizational growth, business development acts as a bond that ties together all the various departments or functions within an organization to help improve and expand sales, product offerings, revenues, talent, brand awareness, and even customer service.

There are many ways that a business development plan can help promote change and affect growth across an organization. Business development is important for building relationships. Regardless of if you are cultivating new talent, networking with potential customers, or courting potential partners, relationship building is an important part of any business development plan. Those who have been in business a number of years can quickly see relationships that will demand the most attention.

Connecting with colleagues, clients, and members of other fundamental networks can help organizations identify new business opportunities and generate leads to make pivotal moves for their organization. As well with good relationships comes the ability to strengthen existing connections for repeat or loyal customers and provide opportunities to enhance the talent working with these relationships. These relationships are key to a strategy for boosting revenues and decreasing costs.

Organizations always look at one of the best ways to boost revenue, and lower cost is through growth. Business development sees growth as its endgame. Growth is one of the most typical metrics for measuring the success of the bottom line. Business development uses a key process of devising a strategy to increase revenue and decrease expenses going out. Focusing on business development can help identify the products and markets that are most successful with the greatest profit potential, allowing the organization to see which objectives to go after first clearly. Yet, business development also means ensuring the decisions that are made keep the costs down and identify areas where growth needs funding to expand.

The overall image of the company can often be improved through business development. Marketing is a key component to an organization's growth, and a key business developer should be skilled at organizing to build a better brand. Business developers also work closely with the marketing and strategy teams to solidify campaigns are hitting the target audience while reaching new markets and potential customers. This is a significant aspect of business development, expanding an organization's reach. Business development leaders use insights to help make informed marketing decisions and guide potential customers to the products and services they will find valuable.

Business development can also tap into areas of opportunity in new markets that are lucrative and trend driven. This means those business developers need to analyze demographics and trends within those demographics, being on top of viral marketing and understanding the difference in influencing customers' correct segments. Let's get started.

Chapter 1: Step 1 - Identify Your Target Market

The business world is one that is in constant change and requires marketers to stay on top of so many moving parts. It also means that organizations must have a well-defined strategy that includes who the target market is. Organizations cannot afford to toss money into the wind and hope it hits the right segments. The wonderful thing is that even small organizations can now effectively compete with larger organizations by focusing on niche markets.

One big mistake that many organizations make is they assume the target market is "anyone interested in the product or service" they provide. Some take it a step further and say, small-business owners, stay-at-home moms, or even homeowners. Yet, all of these are too generalized.

Understand that specific targeting does not exclude those who do not fit your criteria. Instead, it allows the organization to target valuable marketing focus, dollars, and brand message to those with the greatest potential to see value in the products or services the organization offers. When an organization does this, it makes marketing a much more efficient, effective, and affordable process for generating business or reaching clients.

An example of this could be a home décor company that chooses to market to new homeowners between the age of 35 to 55 with an income of $145,000 or greater in Mobile, Alabama. While this seems pretty specific in who the target is, the company could take it even further and target only those interested in bedroom or bathroom decorating in a farmhouse style. The company could then be broken down into two separate segments or niches: parents and those preparing for retirement. As an organization clearly defines the target audience, they find it much easier to see how and where to market.

Understanding Current Customer Base

As an organization clearly defines its target audience, marketing becomes much more effective and easier. To begin doing this taking a look at who the current customers are that the organization services is important. Organizations should understand who the current customers are and why they choose your organization.

Organizations also should look to see if there are any commonalities between customers. Do they have similar characteristics or interests? Which customer is currently bringing more business to the organization? In defining this, the organization can see that it may be possible that others who are like them could see value in the service or product offered.

Who's Shopping the Competition

The next thing that organizations should address is who the competitor targeting is? Who is the current customer they are seeing the highest traction with? Are you targeting the same market? If you are targeting the same customer, take a closer look to see if there is a niche they are overlooking, and your organization could capitalize on it.

What Is Your Service or Product?

Organizations need to understand the products or services they offer. They need to be able to see the features and value that each product provides. So, write out a list of each product and service along with their features. Beside each feature, write the list of benefits that the service or product provides.

An example of this might include the organization offering professional photography services. The photographer offers high-quality image services. This service will attract more customers because they will see the company in a more professional. The ability to have high-quality photography is a benefit to gaining more customers and increasing revenue.

As you identify the benefits listed, the next step is to create a list of those that would benefit from the service. So, when we consider our photographer from the previous example, you could target businesses that are needing to improve their brand recognition to increase their client base. While this is still pretty general, you now have a better understanding of where to begin from.

Considering Demographics to Target

When an organization is considering demographics to target, there are many different areas to consider. When you consider the list of benefits from the previous sections, you next want to look at who is most likely to benefit from the product or service.

Here are some of the factors to consider when developing your list of customers who will benefit:

- Gender
- Age
- Geographic Location
- Income
- Education Level
- Occupation
- Family Status

The key here is to assess who or which group needs the service or value you are providing. Once you have narrowed this down, then you can begin dividing that group further down into smaller niches. To do this, you can consider the group's psychographics. These are

characteristics that are more personal to the target group. These
characteristics include:

- Attitude
- Lifestyle
- Personality
- Values
- Interests
- Behavior
- Hobbies

Again, go back and review how the service or product fits into the
lifestyle of the targeted group. How will the target find value in the
organization's offer? What are the features most appealing to the
target? What media space does the target live in? Does the target
spend more time online, at events, or elsewhere?

Decision Evaluation

So, once you have ironed out a market segment to target, you next
need to consider some additional questions.

- How big is the group that fits into my criteria? Is the segment
  large enough?
- What value will the target get from the product or service?
  Will the need be obvious to the target?

- What drives the decision making for the target?
- Is the product or service at a price the target will accept?
- In what ways can the target be reached with my message? Will it be easy for them to access?

It is important to not break the target down too far; you want to ensure that your niche is large enough to facilitate business growth. Remember, organizations can also have more than one niche market to focus on. This is where the marketers will consider the different messages that will resonate with the different segments. If you can reach a few niches effectively with the same message, then you might have broken the market down too far. As well, if you find that the niche is fifty people or less that fit the criteria, then it is time to reevaluate your target. The trick is to find the perfect balance of showing value to a group and targeting specific groups with your message.

So, the next question is, how do you find out the information that will help you reach your target? The simplest way to start is by doing an online search to research what others have identified about your target. Looking through blogs, magazine articles, and the places or things that your target engages with. One location that can prove to be very insightful for gaining information about your target audience is social media. Once you have identified what network your target audience is living on, you can then go and see how they are interacting. How are they communicating their opinions about brands or products? Look for their comments on your brand's social pages. You can even create your own survey to see what they are looking for and gather feedback.

Defining a target market can be a very challenging part of business development. However, once you know this target, you are equipped with a wealth of information and can make growing your business happen more efficiently. Rather than using a shotgun approach to market to everyone in a specific ZIP code, you can save time and money and market just to those who fit the criteria within your target, saving you time, effort, and valuable budget dollars.

Chapter 2: Step 2 - Identify the Type of Business You Are Running

A big part of business development is understanding the type of business your organization is. Think of it like this you are booking a cruise for you and a partner. Chances are there is a budget to consider, but it is easy to get caught up in the promise of adventure and excursions. I mean, it's a vacation, so why not make it the best possible?

The thought process you go through for something personal versus the thought process you use for something business-related is quite different. I mean, we do not often consider what the return on the investment will be with our personal vacations. However, when we make a business purchase, this is often one of the biggest considerations.

This is why B2C and B2B are fundamentally different when considering the marketing tactics. Understanding the differences is crucial to business development and finding best practices for your organization. When you approach a campaign without all the information, you could possibly be missing out on opportunities.

Understanding B2C and B2B

B2C is the business to customer relationship, while B2B is the business-to-business relationship. A B2C business focuses on services and products to sell to customers for personal use. This includes vacations, cars, clothing, garbage removal, and honestly, a seemingly never-ending list. In contrast, B2B is a business that focuses on selling services and products to other businesses. They, more specifically, are looking for the decision-makers in organizations. These types of businesses offer anything from software for restaurants to office trash cans and copiers.

There are some obvious differences between the marketing for B2C and B2B. However, some of the technical best practices will apply to both types of business marketing strategies. These could include retargeting those who have abandoned items in their car or keyword research. Yet, some crucial differences separate the types of business. When it comes to business development, it is essential to understand these differences so that you can improve efficiency and marketing campaigns.

Decision Makers

In both types of business, the marketing needs to be targeted to get results; however, this can be a greater challenge for the B2B brands.

B2C brands have the flexibility to focus on campaigns to reach potential customers who would be interested in the service or product they have. Sometimes even without the theoretical person making the purchase. An example of this would be a woman who sees a necklace she would like, so she sends the link to her partner. This action could result in a sale even though the ad may never have been appealing to the primary person who made the purchase.

Additionally, B2C brands benefit from reaching household decision-makers, especially when it comes to big-ticket sales like cars or vacations. Yet they do not have to exclusively target that member of the household to get the same result. They can show the ad to anyone who might be interested, and they have a fair chance that it will convert to a sale.

In contrast, B2B marketing needs to specifically target a small group or individual within a business. This target is known as the decision-maker. Think of it like this everyone in the office could want new chairs. However, it is only the office manager or upper management that can ultimately make the decision if anyone or everyone gets a new chair, which means that these are the people that specifically need to be targeted to make the sale. B2B often uses a method of targeting by job title.

Decision Making Process

The process for making decisions looks very different when considering something personally or for business. One thing is true for both, though, is that both consumers and businesses want to see what the appeal is and the value it brings immediately or will not be interested in learning more.

Knowing this, it is important to understand that B2B customers often take a significantly longer time to research and evaluate before making a purchase. However, once they get the initial benefits, they often begin to dig in deeper and learn more and evaluate the details. These customers also look for third party reviews and other competing offers for the same product. The stakes are high for businesses, and they have to ensure they are getting the best value for their business and the best product.

In contrast, B2C customers often want to see everything they need as quickly as they can. Honestly, how much research do they need to do on a new shower curtain? They want to see what the reviews are for the product and if any concerns are resonating on social media for the product. This is known as social proof. These customers weigh slightly more on the impact or opinions of others on social media when making immediate purchases.

Conversion Time

Conversion time is a simple concept, but it is significant. B2C customers will be more likely to purchase after seeing a compelling ad quickly. However, B2B customers are frequently going to take a significantly longer approach, which is directly tied to the research and evaluation process.

Consumers who are purchasing for personal use are much more likely to make impulsive decisions on purchases than those making purchases for the business. This is often because businesses have a stricter budget, and there is a greater amount of pressure to make smart purchases the first time. Changing the process for the business is a complicated and time-consuming process. Sometimes these purchases and mean retraining an entire office on new software, which makes it more imperative to get the purchase right the first time. As well many B2B purchases are much larger than that of B2C impulsive buys. Since the purchase is much more expensive, poor purchases can cause the company to not get the desired results.

Underlying Motivation

The underlying motivations for purchases are often different as well for B2B and B2C. Regardless of the type of business, both make purchases because they see a benefit from a service or product in some way. Sometimes these benefits can overlap, like providing comfort or saving time. However, those motivations have differences.

B2C consumers are purchasing to solve a desire or improve a facet of their life in some way. At the same time, B2B consumers are purchasing to solve a problem or improve their bottom line. This is not to say that emotional appeal is not a tactic to use with both types. After all, both are real people. They have needs, wants, and fears that all can be appealed to. The trick is to tie that emotional appeal to the business in some way that shows an improvement to the financial bottom line.

In the end, when they say business is not personal, they naturally are going to be talking about the difference in marketing between B2C and B2B. Someone making purchases based on an ad from social media for an engagement ring is not going to think the same as the CEO choosing a lawyer for their business. As you are able to understand what type of customer you are targeting, you will be able to improve your results and business development.

Chapter 3: Step 3 - Setting Goals

When you consider where your business development it thinks about past performance. Are you happy with where you have come from? Do you see room for growth? You have made it to step three, so chances are you have not hit every goal you thought you wanted. It's okay you are here to understand how to improve your business development. One of the biggest ways you can do that is through setting goals and not just any goal. The thing to understand is that you have to be clear about what you want. You have to understand that your goal needs to be actionable for your business. You need to understand what changes need to occur to make the goal happen. This step is focused on helping you to drive your performance with setting goals that are more meaningful.

Prioritizing Goals

One of the greatest challenges that organizations face is that everything needs to be seemingly accomplished at one time. You have to retain your current customers, find new ones, manage finance, streamline processes, and keep employees motivated – all at the same time. This can be very overwhelming.

The best process for sifting through all of these important aspects of a business to find which are the most important is to use a SWOT analysis. This helps you to be clear about what your organizational strengths, weaknesses, opportunities, and threats are. Let's look at an example of a business that deals with skincare. Within a SWOT analysis, you will identify the following:

Strengths	Weaknesses
• Good Reputation with Customers • Loyal/Repeat Customers • Ideal Location	• Little investment in marketing • Customers only make small purchases
Opportunities	Threats
• Located in a busy area with lots of offices nearby • Instagram Marketing is working for the competition • Wide range of services and products you could market	• There is a cheaper competitor five minutes away • Lease cost is increasing because of popularity in the area

While this is very basic analysis, it is easy to identify some priorities. One important thing is not to choose too many goals. The last thing a brand should do is to spread itself to thin. So, as you are looking at your SWOT analysis, begin by picking three priorities to create goals for. These may include:

- Improving revenue from existing product lines to loyal customers
- Increasing revenue by targeting individuals working in businesses nearby
- Using Instagram to market business and grow a reputation

All three of these are great priorities; however, they are not goals. To make them goals, they need to be specific and measurable so you can take action.

Discuss Goals

To be successful, you need to get those who work with you on board. The people who support your business are valuable assets, and they should be treated as so. When you are defining business goals, it is important to have key stakeholders involved in the goal process.

Those who work for you are a team of individuals making your products or talking to potential customers. The people can help you see what is working and what needs to change. They have an insight into what is holding back business development and where the focus may need to shift to improve your success with the same amount or less effort.

So, once you have completed the SWOT analysis, have the priorities in hand, engage with your employees, and solicit their

140

feedback. They may completely agree with you, or they may have the insight you had not considered. The more your staff feels involved in the process, the more likely you are to get their buy-in to achieve the goals once set.

Making Goals SMART

So now you have your business priorities, and it is time to make them SMART. A smart goal is one that is specific, measurable, achievable, relevant and time bound. Looking back to our example from earlier of our skincare business, let's take one of the priorities and make it a SMART goal – Generating additional revenue by targeting the workers in the nearby offices.

- Specific – Gain fifteen new customers from within a five-minute radius
- Measurable – Review progress by tracking the number of profits and new customers while maintaining current clients
- Achievable – This can be done by creating customized promotions for the nearby offices and networking with office mangers in the individual buildings
- Relevant – These actions will increase the number of customers and improve business development
- Timely – The fifteen new customers will be achieved by the end of the second quarter.

Key Performance Indicators (KPIs)

It is not enough to set SMART goals; you also need to understand where you are throughout the process. This will help you and your team to see how you are converting the goal into measurable aspects of your business.

The most common way that organizations measure their goals is through key performance indicators (KPIs). These are the numbers you track to show that you are actually making strides toward the goal or not. This is also a great motivator for your team to see their successes. When you have established your smart goal, chances are you established a KPI to be tracked.

Looking back to our previous example, the number of new clients from the office buildings would be a performance indicator. This would also mean that the business would need a method for tracking where new clients came from. It is also possible to create a KPI for the number of flyers put out or networking opportunities attended.

It is possible that you will have many different KPIs for the different aspects of your business, like monthly sales targets and even individual KPIs for each team member. When you push KPIs down throughout your team, you can find that they are more likely to achieve goals when they can see the progress towards that goal.

Good Habits Achieve Goals

Just as with anything in life, the better our habits, the better thing will work out. If you want to make something occur, then you need to create a schedule and build habits around, more specifically, good habits around it. Just as if you would like to personally lose weight or have more energy, you would need to include exercise into your schedule, cook healthy meals, drink the appropriate amount of water, and so on. If you want to achieve goals within your business, then you need to treat them the same way. You need to set actions in place to achieve the KPIs on a scheduled process.

Automated processes are a great way to help you stay on track. Using a calendar that both you and your staff can set reminders to is also helpful. Many organizations use a team's environment to organize deadlines, set tasks, and prompt repeat actions. Often successful businesses put the goal somewhere that everyone can see it along with a tracker to allow the team to see the progress towards the goal.

Though identify and reviewing your focus areas, using SMART goals, acknowledging KPIs for tracking your business will be set up with a system to position for success. All of these things are part of ensuring that your business development is on track that the strategies that are going in place will align with the goals and create a whirlwind of success.

Chapter 4: Step 4 - Generating Leads

It is highly likely that you have experienced the interruption at the worst time of the phone ringing only to hear the person on the other end butcher your name with "an important message about the warranty of your toaster." These frustrating interruptions are the reason we dedicated a chapter specifically to lead generation. The previous example is known as inbound lead generation. Unlocking the key to inbound lead generation can prevent your organization from cold calling and annoying potential customers.

To begin, you should first understand what a lead is. Businesses consider a lead any person that indicates an interest in the company's service or product in some form. Most often, business hears from leads following a potential customer submitting personal information from a subscription, trial, or offer.

Take, for example, if you complete an online survey to learn more about how to care for your car. Then a few days later, you begin to receive emails from an auto company that created the survey with information about car care. This process is far less intrusive than those cold calls that interrupt dinner out of the blue. This is an example of what it is like to be a lead from a consumer perspective.

In contrast, from a business perspective, the information that the car care company collected from the survey allows the company to personalize the communication and target the direct needs of the customer. In using this method, it is almost an instant savings for the business because you are not wasting time cold calling.

Another thing to understand about leads is they are part of a broader lifecycle consumers follow as they go from visitor to customer. As well, not all leads are equal – nor are their qualifications the same. You can qualify leads by different types based on the stage of the lifecycle they are in.

There are a few different categories that can qualify leads. First, let's look at marketing qualified leads (MQL) – these leads are contacts that have engaged with the efforts made by the marketing team but are not ready for a sale. An example of this could include a person who filled out a form on a landing page from an offer. Another lead qualification is a sales qualified lead (SQL) – these are contacts that have specifically expressed interest or indicated they are eager to become a paying customer.

The third type of qualification is product qualified leads (PQL), which are contacts that have used the product or service or have taken action to be a paying customer. PQL's could include those who have used a trial product or a limited version or free option with the possibility of upgrading. The last qualification type is a qualified service lead. These contacts are customers that have indicated to the services team of the organization that they are interested in becoming a customer. One example of this would include a customer who tells the service rep that they are looking to upgrade a product they currently subscribe to or use.

Understanding Lead Generation

Let's begin with understanding what lead generation is; it is the process of converting potential customers or strangers into prospects for your business. One way to think of lead generation is to find unique ways to attract people to a business. It is all about finding ways to warm a customer to the idea of doing business with your business.

Businesses need a lead generation to help grow their business development. They have to find ways to get strangers to start relationships with their business. Lead generation falls within the second stage of the customer lifecycle. This is because it occurs after you have attracted the potential customer and are ready to convert the lead into a sale.

Lead Generation Process

So how do you generate leads? There is a basic process for doing this, and it begins with visitors discovering your business through some sort of marketing channel. These marketing channels could include social media, blogs, or websites. Next, the visitor should be drawn to a call-to-action (CTA), which might be an image, message, or button that encourages the potential customer to interact. These CTAs will then drive the potential customer to a landing page.

These types of pages are designed to gather information about the lead in exchange for something in return, like an offer. An offer can look very different depending on the business. It might be an eBook, a template, a course, or even a trial. One key thing to remember is the offer needs to have enough value to make the prospective customer act upon it. While the customer is on the landing page, they then typically complete the form and receive the offer. A form is a great way to gather information about a customer, and they can often be embedded anywhere on your site.

Qualifying Leads

So, we have identified who a lead is as a person who is interested in the company's service or product. The next step is to understand the ways in which someone actually shows interest. The information collection process helps you see just what the individual is interested in. Are they seeking a job, shopping for a good or service, looking for a coupon, or downloading something educational? As you answer these questions, you can then define where they are and what type of lead they are.

You will also want to gauge the lead's level of interest. There are many ways you can gauge just how interested someone is. Lead scoring is one method that many brands use to quantify the lead with a numerical value. With this method, they assign a score to see how interested or ready for sale the lead is. The great thing about this is the criteria is up to your company. The one catch is that the criteria must be uniform across the sales and marketing departments so that all departments are working on the same scale.

Some things that may be considered in a lead's score would include information they shared, engagement level with the brand, actions they have taken, or other criteria you have deemed as important to the lead. So, if a lead had inquired about a coupon, that action would likely increase their score because they are actively interested in the product.

The greater the lead score, the closer they should be to making the purchase. The criteria you use will likely need to be tweaked as you progress until you find the perfect formula for your brand. However, once you unlock that formula, your quality of lead generation to customer conversion will greatly change.

Chapter 5: Step 5 - Increasing Website Traffic

It is likely that you have heard about search engine optimization or SEO and how it can increase the traffic that is generated to your website. However, there are other ways to increase your website traffic other than SEO. Using search engines should not be your only form of driving traffic to your website; it actually can be bad for your organization if it is the only way you are getting traffic.

Knowing how to diversify the traffic to your site means you are not singly relying on SEO. The biggest reason you want to diversify is that if your primary source of traffic fails, it could be detrimental to your business. So, for this step, we are going to consider the different options on how you can increase traffic without relying on SEO.

Considering Traffic

One thing that is important to remember is that not all traffic to your site is equally valuable. One thing that every brand strives for is high-quality traffic. High-quality traffic generates a better ROI and is laser targeted and generates a better ROI than other traffic.

Of course, it might sound great to drive high traffic to your site; however, if that traffic is not converting to sales, then high traffic numbers are not a great tool for your website. High traffic numbers are good, do not get me wrong, but it can become just a vanity metric. This is important to keep in mind as we consider traffic. If you have 10,000 visits to your site, but they are not targeted is by far not the same as 1,000 targeted visits driven to your site. Effective traffic most often will have a prior interest in the product or service you offer and is ready to spend on a similar solution.

The top areas to drive traffic that is targeted include eCommerce sites and from search engines. However, you cannot discount the traffic you can drive from social media. One thing that is important to consider is what your audience's social profile looks like. Is this profile active on social media? It is possible to drive a significant amount of targeted traffic from social media with the correct strategy.

Take, for example, the targeted segment of millennials who pretty much live on social media. Brands that have a goal to reach this type of segment would benefit most from content that is share-worthy. One way that businesses have found great success in driving traffic to their site is through the use of video. A high-quality, quick video that can be easily distributed across social media channels to create awareness. To do this, businesses are using a social advertising model. It works much better than word-of-mouth and helps them connect with more audiences.

Online Advertising

It is possible to generate hundreds, if not thousands of clicks to your site with online ads. One good thing about the digital world is that there frequently are new social platforms and ad options appearing and innovating. With all this innovation, it makes getting ads in front of your target market easier than ever. One of the keys to business development is knowing the effectiveness of online advertising. There is so much power in using social media as a method for online advertising. Chances are your organization does not have a bottomless pit of money. This is okay because if you are effective on social media, you do not need a ton of money to see ROI from the ads you place.

So, the challenge of online advertising can be broken down into two ingredients. The first ingredient is having a product or service that people want. Then you combine a high-quality ad that people want to click on or share for the second ingredient. It would be impossible to discuss all the products that people could want here. However, it is possible to discuss what it takes to create a high-quality ad. That will work on social media and search engines.

There are generally a few things to know when creating ads first, who you are targeting, and second, the design of the ad. Design can include the verbiage as well as the image or artwork. If you want quality designed ads that generate traction, one thing many brands do is to study what ads the competition is running and what is working for them. Often tools to gather information about the performance of your competitor's ads are hidden right in front of you.

One example of this is on Facebook. If you click the down arrow at the top right corner of an ad, you can choose, "Why am I seeing this?" Facebook will then give your insight into how that ad was chosen for you. These insights are based on interests, geography, demographics, and can be very precise.

Another trick that many businesses do is they are subscribed to the competition's email list. This allows them to get information that the brand is sending out directly to their targeted market. Through the process of studying these ads, you can see the competitor's success and begin to emulate that success for yourself. Thus, saving your company valuable research time and effort. Another pro tip is to create a swipe file; this is basically a record of ads that are eye-catching and caused you as a consumer to take action.

Targeting
Regardless of the ad platform, they each offer a form of targeting. To be successful at this, you will need to do some research ahead of time for the platform that you want to drive success with. Let's say you are targeting a specific segment of your audience that is converting better than another. Many platforms allow you to create a Lookalike audience to close that high-converting audience and deliver ads to similar people to that segment. As well you can also select a

percentage that you want to reach. Facebook is one platform that allows you a significant amount of flexibility with your targeting choices.

For brands that have a diverse offering, it is a great option to use custom audiences. This allows you to create audiences and ad content based on the segments you want to reach. It also helps you to avoid spending on promoting your site to people who would not be interested.

Guest Blogging

Another option or generating visitors to your site is guest blogging. One very effective option for driving traffic to your site is through guest blogging. Depending on your organization, it can be the lifeblood of your digital presence. There are a few things that you must get correct when it comes to guest blogging. When you are looking to do this for your organization, you want to first find sites that are suited for your nice and that accept guest posting. This can be done as simple as doing a quick google search. The key formula here is to search using this format:

- (your niche) + (search string)

Search strings should include: guest post, contributing writer, guest posting guidelines, suggested post, contributor guidelines, guest post wanted, writers wanted, write for us.

So, your search might look:

- Name of niche + write for us

The next important thing that you must be able to do is to write compelling content that others would want to share on their site. Great content is important to strengthen your brand. When paired with the right target audience, this is a powerful tool.

Blog commenting

Another tactic that brands also employ is blog commenting to drive traffic to their site. To do this, you first need to find sites that are producing content that is related to your niche. One thing to keep in mind is that you will need to be able to commit a significant amount of time to blog commenting. With this method, you also must remember that persistence is important, as well as commenting first on the post. As well keep in mind that comments left on industry-specific sites will generally result in a higher related return in traffic on your site. However, it is best to avoid commenting on a competitor's blog; this might seem rude and have a negative effect on your brand.

It is also important to make sure your comment has merit or continues the discussion. Simply posting a "Nice website" or "Great post" does not add value for other readers and will not help you get the results you are looking for. One great thing to look for is when someone posts a question, providing an answer that is thorough and thoughtful shows readers that you are engaged. It can also showcase that you have expertise in the subject or with the niche. This encourages those reading to click your name and be taken to your own site.

Even if the subject is one that you are not very familiar with, you should include your own thoughts. For these situations, it is a great opportunity to ask questions. Then the author would be able to elaborate on the more complexities of the topic when it is a subject you are knowledgeable feel free to contribute. Keeping in mind that powerful questions can drive traffic back to your site.

One error that many brands make is they embed links into their comments. This comes off as spammy and is a turn off for readers. This is why it is important that you have linked your URL in your profile so that traffic can be driven back to your blog or site from your comments. As well you do not want to use the name of your business as you are commenting, you will gain more trust by using your own name. You have to think of this process as a relationship building. You wouldn't walk up to a stranger and insert your product or service; first, you would begin with a hello and sharing who you are.

Chapter 6: Step 6 - Using Sales Funnels

Business development means growing and adapting. It also is good to plan in your business some options for sales funnels. By now, you understand that the sales process is not a straight line. Getting a lead to a customer often takes its own course, and it can differ depending on the business. Regardless of if you are a B2B or B2C company, it is important that the sales department understand the journey that consumers will go on. If they do not understand this, they are just shooting in the dark as they are trying to reach goals. This process dates back to the 1890s and still applies today; it is called a sales funnel.

Understanding a Sales Funnel

As a prospect becomes a customer, they will go through different stages; a sales funnel provides an illustration of that process. This process resembles an inverted pyramid. The pyramid starts with a lot of potential customers at the top. Then the sales department will engage with them and narrow down the most qualified prospects moving them to the next stage until ultimately they close at the bottom of the funnel. The sales funnel and buying process are the two sides of the buying process. However, the sales funnel is more the perspective of the buyer, not the seller. This process is broken down into awareness, consideration, and decision.

Awareness is the top portion of the funnel. This is where the buyer identifies that there is a problem or issue they need to solve. They begin to look for solutions and discover services or products that can solve the problem. The middle of the funnel is consideration; this is where the buyer is spending time evaluating different channels. They also will begin engaging with sellers or those who offer a solution to their problem or need. The bottom area of the funnel is decision, which is where the buyer decided on the solution for his or her problem and makes a purchase of a good or service to solve it.

While there are distinct differences in the sales funnel and the buyer's journey, they have concepts that overlap. This happens when the buyer enters the consideration stage of the funnel. It is at this point that the buyer journey aligns with the sales process.

Sales Funnel Management

A sales funnel is the process in which leads travel through your organization's sales process from start to finish. This is a basic visual representation of the numbers in the form of a funnel. However, there is more to it than just visuals. As you can analyze the number of leads entering the funnel and the number of conversions to a customer, you can find that there is a significant dip. Often prospects drop out the sides of your funnel when the product or service does not match their needs. This is okay because it is nearly impossible to retain every prospect who enters your funnel. Nevertheless, it is important that your sales department make efforts to retain the ones who are ready to purchase.

Yet, given the number of leads that fill your funnel, the sales department can often have trouble converting if they cannot tell the difference between a hot or cold lead. As a result, unqualified hot leads at the top of the funnel may drop out due to slow response time or other lack of connection with the sales team. As a business, this is not good for business development and can be seen as a leak in your funnel. There are actually many ways that leads can leak out of your funnel.

So how do you spot and stop the leaks in order to take advantage of these potential leads and capture this revenue in your funnel? First, you want to make sure you are using a sales funnel software like a Customer Relations Management (CRM), where you can qualify leads quickly, track their activity, and follow-up automatically at the correct time.

The adoption of a CRM within your sales funnel management impacts the performance of your sales department in a positive way. However, what happens with some is they fail to realize that it is more than just a customer database; CRM can be the most beneficial tool for managing sales that the department has. This process helps the sales department to define the sales process and identify where leaks are happening. As well, it helps to streamline conversions and bring leads down the funnel more efficiently.

Developing a Sales Funnel

Regardless if you are automating emails or defining your funnel stages, you can set your sales to funnel software to help the sales department advance leads and stop the loss of hot leads.

You will begin with organizing leads as they come into the funnel. This is one of the processes that a sales funnel software speeds up the sales process. As data is organized, it is easier to break it down into modules for managing opportunities, leads, and customers. The first step in the sales process is to capture leads. Some funnels use software that captures leads as they visit your site through submitting a form or emailing the company. This makes it easier for sales to know who to start working with instead of wasting time on data entry. Many CRMs can also segment leads based on criteria the sales department predefines and then send automatically assign the lead to the correct sales rep.

As a lead enters the CRM, it is marked with a segment of "new." This happens to every lead at the top stage of the funnel. As a sales rep works with the leads, they then begin to subsequently move to the next stages. Using filter views in the software, the sales reps can reveal the number of leads at each stage in the funnel. They can also see how many have engaged with reps, how many are at the bottom of the funnel, and how many are ready to close. This knowledge is actionable and very valuable to see how your sales strategies are being successful.

Qualifying Leads Within the Funnel

One of the biggest challenges that is found and very important to the growth of your business development is that the sales department must be able to identify qualified leads. Those who have been in sales for a significant time often can qualify their leads over time; they know it almost naturally. However, this process is not as effective or efficient if they do not know the right opportunities to qualify. This can become a major issue if you have a young or very new sales department. They can often struggle with picking out which leads are qualified in the funnel and then feel forced to chase all the leads. Eventually getting burnt out and getting nowhere in the process.

Software for sales funnels is increasingly intelligent. As artificial intelligence continues to grow in strength, the software now has the ability to qualify the lead based on properties that the sales department. These properties can include interest, behaviors, and really anything that the sales department would find valuable. This saves sales valuable time and money, scrambling to see if the lead is qualified or not. It helps the sales to also identify leads that are hot, cold, or warm and create an effective lead scoring system.

In many sales funnel software, you can configure lead scoring rules to make the ideal buyer by simply adding or subtracting points from the properties of the lead. An example of this could be: assume that your business is predominately local. A metric for the software may include criteria that the customer must live within the servicing area of your business and assign their location 20 points. If the lead is not within the service area, then it may subtract 10 points. You basically can add and subtract scores for all kinds of things, did the enter an email address, phone number, and so on. Then you bring everything together and quantify that lead as cold, warm, or hot in the sales funnel for your reps to be able to close more deals at a quicker pace.

Engaging Leads Through the Funnel

Once leads have been scored and organized, the next step is for the sales department to reach out to those priority leads using email or phone. Tracking conversations should be a priority for your sales department. Knowing when they last emailed or had a phone conversation is great, but it is not enough. They should also know what they spoke about and have a strategic plan for the next conversation.

Many organizations still are using separate tools for email and calling leads; when this happens, it is harder to visualize the different touchpoints at different stages. When an organization is using a sales funnel software with built-in features of the phone and email, this visualization happens seamlessly. This process allows organizations to create template emails in the funnel software to be able to more efficiently and quickly reach out to leads. Additionally, many of the beginning emails can be automated and send out welcome emails to new leads based on workflows already set up.

The more modern CRMs also allow the tracking of emails and notifications for when those leads open an email. This is a great feature for sales reps because they know when to take action and move the lead to the next step of the process. In sales, it is important to strike when the lead is hot. So, knowing when or if the email is getting read is very important. This can also be a metric that helps the organization test how successful email performance is and craft better options to increase open rates.

As the world has become more and more digital, it is important to remember that the phone is still a highly effective tool for sales reps to sell with. This is why it is highly recommended that there be a phone in your CRM and that your stales team capitalizes on this feature to call leads. A productive CRM takes the hassle out of making calls and allows the salesperson to use a single click to make calls, record calls, and log calls without the need for any third-party tools.

Automation of Moving Leads Within the Funnel

One benefit of good sales funnels management is the ability to be consistent in updating the lead stage. As leads progress down the funnel, users need to be able to analyze the number of leads at every stage and ensure that the funnel is always staying full from top to bottom. It is also essential to know what stage each lead is at a quick glance; when you can quickly identify where a lead is at within the funnel, the rep knows what to do next. When the CRM has the ability to move the lead along the funnel process automatically, it helps the sales team save time.

Let me be very clear on something leads will not move down the funnel on their own. Sales reps will have to continue to do their party of selling and qualifying to allow them to move through the funnel. The software, however, can update based on actions that the rep sets in place. This workflow automation helps the lead progress based on the work that the sales rep is doing. This is where it becomes increasingly important to remember to update the sales stage as they progress. When reps are using a CRM, the software is able to fill gaps within the automation rather than relying on the mental ability of the rep to move a person through the process manually.

Key Sales Funnel Metrics

There are many metrics that identify a good CRM; however, the following are some key metrics to track.

Lead Velocity Rate

Lead velocity rate is a metric that refers specifically to qualified lead growth, month-on-month. It measures the number of leads the organization is currently working on converting to customers. Organizations use this metric as a real-time indicator of sales revenue and growth. So, if the lead velocity rate is high, then the organization should expect high sales revenue to be high as well.

Conversion Rate

The conversion rate is a measurement of how successful the sales department is converting leads. How well these leads are converting is imperative to see if the sales reps are getting quality leads, and if the individual reps are performing at their optimum level. With software for sales funnels, organizations can create funnel reports to show how the leads are converting at different stages and by which members of the sales department. They can even report on how they are converting by sales campaign as well. This information and the ability to analyze which leads are moving and converting allows the organization to review the strategies in place for better conversion.

Opportunity Count

Opportunity count is exactly what you think it is. It is the total number of opportunities across the individual stages of the sales funnel. With this metric, you want to see that you have a good balance of leads within each stage of the funnel. If you notice that there is an excessive amount of leads at a specific stage, that could indicate that there is an issue that the reps are struggling with. This could very well be a red flag, and you should assess what needs to be changed to help move the leads down the funnel.

Duration in Stage

It makes sense to think that minimizing the time a lead spends in each stage of the process is a good thing. Shortening the length of the average sales cycle could be a good thing. It is important that you remind the sales department that they should use discretion when doing this. Often in a rush to convert leads to the next step, they could lose the lead. No one likes a sales rep that is too aggressive or pushy. The sales department should remember that the lead is coming to them to solve a problem, moving too quickly could ultimately backfire on them.

Chapter 7: Step 7 - Viral Marketing

The idea of your business going viral is one that is exciting and a desire of many organizations. Obviously, you want to get your name in front of as many people as possible. In fact, raising brand awareness is the number one goal among many looking to improve brand development? This one of the key reasons that many businesses look to viral marketing as an opportunity to launch into super fandom. But what is viral marketing?

Understanding viral marketing begins with understanding it in a simple definition. Viral marketing is a marketing promotion that relies on the audience generating the message of the service or product. This is that the marketing is considered to be viral when it reaches the point where the public is sharing it at a larger rate than just the target audience. When this is achieved, the message will reach nearly every social media platform and nearly all users.

Understating How Viral Marketing Works

The easiest way to illustrate how viral marketing works is similar to that of the popularity of memes. Although memes are not specifically tied to a product, the way they spread goes hand in hand with the principles of the way viral marketing spreads.

Think for a moment about something seemingly random that seems to take over your social feeds from nowhere. Memes get promoted and shared like crazy because they resonate with people, including the outsiders who involve themselves with these random phenomenal trends with likes or shares. The same rules apply when it comes to viral marketing. In these instances, customers or followers share the content because the ad or message was buzz worthy.

Examples of Viral Marketing

Understanding what viral marketing looks like can be helpful when looking at some examples of it in real-world action. One great example of this is Dollar Shave Club (DSC) who broke out in 2012 with their marking campaign, "Our Blades Are F***ing Great." Before this campaign, the company was a relatively small direct sales company that was unknown but an up-and-comer in the subscription shaving space. Through the use of this unconventional and funny video ad, the company racked up tens of millions of views quickly on YouTube then quickly making the rounds on social media. In a short few months, the DSC subscriptions and interest had spiked and was highlighted by Google Trends. This became one of the most well-documented examples of viral marketing.

With the use of self-aware and funny-focus advertising being adopted by more organizations over the years, restaurants and brands like MoonPie, Denny's, and Wendy's began to regularly publish memes and tweets that went viral because of their humor. Another great example of this would include the 2018 campaign of IHOP with the brand temporarily deeming themselves the "International House of Burgers" (IHOB). While the brand received a lot of criticism for the bait-and-switch, the numbers did not lie. The use of viral marketing in this campaign produced results that made it into mainstream media attention.

It's also important to note that not all viral marketing campaigns are light-hearted or funny. Popular campaigns over the years would also include Always "Like a Girl" ad, Gillette's "Be a Man," or the ALS Ice Bucket Challenge, which took serious issues and created social stigmas. The popularity of these ads generated the concept that brands were getting real and speaking from a place of authenticity as a key element of getting their message to spread.

Commonality in Viral Marketing Campaigns
Viral content and messages vary broadly from business to business; there are, however, a few elements that these campaigns share. These are important to understand when determining if the campaign has the potential to go viral or even just create serious buzz.

Organic
It is important to understand that you cannot force a campaign to go viral. They have to happen organically. Just as with any trend,

whether or not something gets shared is ultimately up to the audience who views it. Content that spreads organically is how viral marketing works. Honestly, it sometimes is just about placing the right content at the right time in the right place. Just as memes and crazes are difficult to define, you cannot always easily predict viral marketing. However, with that being said, marketers can work to set content for sharing by understanding the pulse on social media and the trends that are happening.

Timely

Timing is something that happens; just as with trends, things come, and things go. While viral marketing campaigns have the potential to leave an impression. It is important to understand that people have a really short attention span for these types of hot topics, memes, and trends. Often, by the time a trend is full-blown, people are often looking for the next big thing.

It is also important that companies refrain from simply attempting to repeat another viral campaign. Just because something is hot right now does not mean that it will have staying power.

Bold

The use of viral marketing campaigns and tactics comes along with big risks involved. Going viral means doing something that grabs the attention of not just your followers but the public. This doesn't always happen by accident, and it rarely happens by playing it safe.

Going back to the example from DSC's bold add "Our Blades Are F***ing Great," this was a big risk that paid off. However, it could easily have been received as too edgy or trying too hard. Likewise, had the same ad come out today, it might not have had as much an impact. It is important to understand it is not necessary that the campaign be controversial. However, they often tend to come from left field, which brings us to the downside of viral marking, going viral for the wrong reason. Some of these include Kylie Jenner's 2017 Pepsi ad or the Rick and Morty promotion of McDonald's in 2018. Both great examples of taking things too far the wrong way.

How to Start with Viral Marketing

When considering your business development, the marketing teams are looking for concrete RO! From their time spent marketing. This includes that time spent on social media. This means that often going after viral moments rather than looking big picture is not a top priority for the majority of businesses.

Nevertheless, there are takeaways and tips that all brands can take from viral marketing regardless of the size and shape of the business. The biggest benefit is staying in touch with the audience and what they are in too. As well, the brand should be reacting in a way that furthers and fits within the brand's identity. The marketing team should have a handle on what content is buzz-worthy and sharable. Those brands looking to produce content that is share-worthy and increase their presence in the social world should focus on these pro-tips.

Pro-Tip 1: Why Do You Want to Go Viral in the First Place?

One of the greatest obstacles that companies are attempting to go viral face is not knowing why they want to be in everyone's social feed. Is it brand awareness, improving your mentions, or catching the eye of potential customers? Organizations must alight their viral attempts with an overall goal. This process will provide a guide toward creating meaningful content rather than just throwing something out there and hoping that social picks it up and runs. Just as with any part of the business, you have to have a plan of action to go along with the content, and campaigns that are viral are no different.

Pro-Tip 2: Understand Social Media Reporting

The audience plays a pivotal role in what gets shared; you have heard that time and time again. The audience matters. If you are looking to create content, then you need to know what is resonating with the followers you currently have. You figure that out through understanding what parts of your content is performing the best by monitoring specific social media metrics. These metrics include things like keyword traffic, audience engagement, clicks and reach, page impressions, and demographic data. Nearly all social networks offer some standard metrics to provide insight into what content is most likely to be shared; this could be videos; it could be memes.

Regardless, it means that organizations must put time and effort into social media analytics.

Pro-Tip 3: Content Must Be Primed to Share

Okay, yes, this seems like a trivial tip. However, you have to make sure the content is optimized for quick sharing easily. It is important that you understand that social campaigns should not only be confined to the business's main account. Regardless of if this is a blog, newsletter, event, you need to consider how far you can spread the message to what is available to you.

After you have considered how far you can spread, then brainstorm the best social media platforms for your promotion or content to live on. If it is image-based content, then Instagram might be the best choice; if it is video-based, then maybe YouTube or TikTok.

Nevertheless, if you truly want to go viral, you should make the sharing across platforms as seamless as possible. When you do this, you need to make sure your audience has the easiest routes to share for your campaign. To make things easy for the audience, you should do the following.

- Make available different routes to share
- Offer a giveaway of a Free service or product
- Acknowledge a key motivation for your audience

- Ask questions improving engagement with viewers or fans
- Do not gate content.

Pro-Tip 4: Hashtags

Social sharing and hashtags go together hand in and. Hashtags are an amazing tool to bring awareness and easy sharing of campaigns. The use of hashtags can make the content more visible and memorable to the audience. Businesses that take the time to develop a hashtag that is worthwhile can track success from that campaign based on the shares and mentions of that hashtag. As well, there are many options for brands to uncover hashtag analytics and find what hashtags are relevant to the target audience, and measure the performance of brand-specific hashtags.

Pro-Tip 5: Trend-jacking

One of the easiest ways to grow your brand awareness without the process of going viral yourself is through trend-jacking. This process is a piggybacking your brand onto a meme or some pop culture trend that is already going viral. This has become more and more present, and a staple in marketing practices as the viral market grows. Businesses that are using social listening can tap quickly into these types of real-time trends and understand how they are relevant to the organization's target audience.

Pro-Tip 6: Humanize

This is as simple and straightforward as it can be, and honestly, one of the most important tips. The most common thread between viral content is that they are human. This is saying that they are organic, relatable, and personable. The growth in authentic marketing is essential to reach the next generations of customers. Brands that are seeing the most engagement and shares are those whose content is humanized and seems genuine from the brand. Stripping the corporate glitz and taste of the content is a plus when it comes to viral marketing.

Conclusion

So, this brings us to an end; *Business Development* is an act of growing and developing an organization as a whole. Many of the techniques and processes for business development mean including those across the business, making departments move from a siloed approach to a bigger picture thinking. The core responsibility of business development is the growth of the business. It is with additional strategies and responsibilities that the organization can accomplish large goals and ideally move the organization to the best possible position.

Defining a business development strategy is an integral part of any organization's growth and success. However, the concept of "business development" is somewhat different for different people. If you ask twelve people what business development is, you will likely end up with twelve different answers. This is largely due to the role of business development changes and grows as the organization grows and changes. The role also will be different based on the age, priority, maturity, and size of the organization.

The overall image of the company can often be improved through business development. Marketing is a key component to an organization's growth, and a key business developer should be skilled at organizing to build a better brand. Business developers also work closely with the marketing and strategy teams to solidify campaigns are hitting the target audience while reaching new markets and potential customers. This is a significant aspect of business development, expanding an organization's reach. Business development leaders use insights to help make informed marketing decisions and guide potential customers to the products and services they will find valuable.

Business development can also tap into areas of opportunity in new markets that are lucrative and trend driven. This means those business developers need to analyze demographics and trends within those demographics, being on top of viral marketing and understanding the difference in influencing customers' correct segments.

As you finish up *Business Development,* you are now armed with so much information to go out into the world and develop strategic plans for marketing and your organizations as a whole. The organization that you serve will be all the better for having you as part of their teams. It is with your growth in knowledge and application of the steps taught within this guide that you will be vastly ahead of the competition. As the industry or marketplace, the brands you work with change, remember it is about adapting and saying true to the value you can provide your stakeholders.

More by Santino Spencer

Discover all books from the Marketing Management Series by Santino Spencer at:

bit.ly/santino-spencer

Book 1: Marketing Strategy

Book 2: Business Branding

Book 3: Digital Marketing

Book 4: Social Media Marketing

Book 5: Marketing Analytics

Book 6: Content Marketing

Book 7: Business Development

Book 8: Mobile Marketing

Themed book bundles available at discounted prices:

bit.ly/santino-spencer

www.ingramcontent.com/pod-product-compliance
Lightning Source LLC
Chambersburg PA
CBHW071155050326
40689CB00011B/2125